ALSO BY GRANT GOLLIHER

Chasing a Dream: A Horseman's Memoir

Think Like a Horse

a Horse

Lessons in Life, Leadership,
and Empathy from an
Unconventional Cowboy

Grant Golliher
with Ellen Daly

G. P. Putnam's Sons
New York

PUTNAM
— EST. 1838 —

G. P. Putnam's Sons
Publishers Since 1838
An imprint of Penguin Random House LLC
penguinrandomhouse.com

Copyright © 2022 by Unbridled Horses, LLC

A listing of photo credits can be found on p. 254.

Library of Congress Control Number: 2022934612

Hardcover ISBN: 9780593331927
Ebook ISBN: 9780593331934

Printed in the United States of America
1st Printing

Book design by Tiffany Estreicher

This is a work of nonfiction. Some names and identifying details have been changed.

To the next generation of leaders

CONTENTS

INTRODUCTION

All I Really Need to Know I Learned from a Horse · 1

CHAPTER ONE

You Can't Lie to a Horse · 15

CHAPTER TWO

Feel Can't Be Taught, but It Can Be Learned · 35

CHAPTER THREE

Give Him the Name You Want Him to Live Up To · 53

CHAPTER FOUR

Clear Boundaries Make Happy Horses · 71

CHAPTER FIVE

Make the Right Thing Easy and
the Wrong Thing Difficult · 97

CHAPTER SIX

Slow to Take and Quick to Give · 113

Contents

CHAPTER SEVEN

It's Not About Today, It's About the Rest of Her Life · 137

CHAPTER EIGHT

If You Deal with an Attitude, You
Won't Have to Deal with an Action · 155

CHAPTER NINE

You Can Be Bitter or You Can Be Better · 173

CHAPTER TEN

Don't Be Afraid to Move Your Feet · 189

CHAPTER ELEVEN

Every Horse Needs a Purpose · 211

CHAPTER TWELVE

Show Your Other Side · 233

Acknowledgments · 252
Photo Credits · 254
Index · 255

Think Like a Horse

All I Really Need to Know I Learned from a Horse

"I understand you help people who've got horse problems."
"No ma'am, I don't. . . . It's kind of the other way around.
I help horses who've got people problems."

—Nɪᴄʜᴏʟᴀs Evᴀɴs,
The Horse Whisperer

G ROWING UP, my best friends had four legs and big ears. My dad raised mules on our peach farm in Palisade, a small town in western Colorado where the Rockies give way to the Utah desert.

At the age of eleven, I was tasked with "breaking" the mule colts—the old cowboy term for teaching a horse to accept a saddle, a bridle, and a rider. As the term implies, it's not typically done gently. The idea is to break the will of the much larger and stronger animal so that he will submit to the direction of his rider. Or, as my dad put it: "Show 'em who's boss."

I could feel the colts' fear as Dad held them tightly by the halter rope. I'd scramble onto their backs and hang on for dear life as they panicked and bolted through the peach trees. It's little wonder they were afraid. For a horse in the wild, the only thing likely to land on its back is a mountain lion. I was afraid, too, with good reason. I soon had plenty of cuts and bruises where I'd been raked under a tree or dumped on the hard ground with the wind knocked out of me, gasping for air.

I quickly learned something important about a mule. You can't make him do something if he thinks he's going to get hurt. Especially not if you're a scrawny kid weighing less than sixty pounds. So I'd need to figure out how to cooperate with them instead. Plus, I didn't like the way my dad's training methods relied on pain and fear.

"Kick them in the belly to get their attention," he'd say.

That didn't sit right with me. So instead, I tried to befriend the mules, get inside their heads, and figure out how to convince them to cooperate. One of the first tricks I learned with my favorite colt, Skeeter, was that if I scratched him behind his big yellow ears, he'd lower his head for more and I could quietly swing a leg over his neck. Then, when he raised his head again, I'd slide down and be sitting on his back. I rode him without saddle or bridle, and when I wanted him to stop, I'd just lean forward and clasp my arms around his neck.

These days, I mount my horses in a more conventional manner. But the basic principles I employed with those mules—trust, patience, firmness, kindness, and respect—are still the foundation of my life's work. And not just with my four-legged friends, but with two-legged ones as well.

It turns out that thinking like a horse can teach you a lot about being a human being.

A Student of the Horse

If you'd told me back then that I'd end up focusing my work not just on horses but on people, I would never have believed you. The last thing I could have imagined is that I'd end up writing books and teaching leadership principles to executives, coaches, parents, politicians, judges, and more. My boyhood dream was to become a mountain man like the legendary figures in the books I loved. I would live alone out in the wilderness with my mules—hunting, fishing, and trapping. I was always more content with animals than with other human beings.

This makes sense when I think about my childhood experiences. My mother battled suicidal depression and sought comfort in God. My dad, in those early days, was a harsh man who had no idea how to give or receive affection. He was never physically abusive to me or any of my three siblings, but he was very critical, and he had little time or patience for his kids. I grew up largely unsupervised, to a degree that I now understand bordered on neglect. There was no one stopping me from swimming in the fast-flowing irrigation canal, riding up treacherous cliff paths on the high mesas, and camping out in the wilderness with only my mules for company. At the age of nineteen, I saddled up one mule, Kate, loaded my packs on another mule, Jack, and set off on a journey north along the Continental Divide toward Canada.

I only made it as far as Wyoming, where I got work on a

ranch and started living the cowboy life. It was there that I met my first wife, Locke, a talented horsewoman and musician. Together, we lived and worked at international polo clubs and on ranches from Texas to California to Kansas to Idaho and eventually back to Wyoming. My love of horses never wavered, and I was considered a good trainer, but I mostly did things the old way, which relied on force, fear, intimidation, and repetition. I wasn't intentionally cruel—people who work with horses in this way generally are not—but I was no longer a boy making friends with his mules. I'd lost touch with that natural sensitivity I once had. Horses were my livelihood, and I did whatever seemed necessary to produce well-trained, obedient mounts for the ranch, the polo field, or the show ring. I'd not yet learned how to think like a horse.

Everything changed for me when I was introduced to a horse trainer by the name of Ray Hunt. Ray reminded me what Skeeter the mule had taught me: that introducing a horse to a saddle and a rider doesn't have to involve breaking his will. In fact, it can be done with the very opposite approach: allowing the horse to exercise his free will, and creating a situation in which he *chooses* to cooperate with his rider.

Some call this horse-led approach "natural horsemanship." Others call it "horse whispering." It's not really as mysterious as it sounds. It just means understanding how the horse's mind works and then using that knowledge to cultivate a willing partnership based on mutual trust and respect, fairness, and clear boundaries. In other words, thinking like a horse. It's a form of subtle communication that takes place through body language and the skillful application of pressure and release. It's so effective it can seem like magic, but it actually comes down to applying a few simple principles consistently.

Using the philosophy I learned from Ray, and later from his mentor Tom Dorrance and another great horseman, Tink Elordi, I became a student of the horse once again. After Locke and I separated, I eventually met Jane, who would become my second wife. My daughter, Tara, and I moved to Wyoming to live on the Diamond Cross Ranch, just north of Jackson Hole, at the foot of the Tetons. As I always say, I'm the lucky cowboy that showed up and married the rancher's daughter. This beautiful piece of land, and the safe harbor I found in my marriage, would become the setting for me to find my true calling in life.

It started almost by accident. Jane and I were asked if we were interested in putting on a private rodeo to entertain three hundred executives from Microsoft. We hired local cowboys to ride bulls and bucking horses and to compete in barrel racing. The audience loved it, and we made more money in one night than we made in a whole summer riding colts. Other groups followed. I began including demonstrations of "horse whispering" in the events—using the principles I'll share with you in this book—and the response was unexpected. It turned out that what people got out of these little exhibitions was far more than mere entertainment. We received a flurry of messages telling us how powerful the impact had been, both personally and professionally.

"I didn't just learn how to be a better leader, I learned how to be a better parent," wrote one CEO.

"It's really changed the way I interact with my team," a

manager reported. "I've learned to be less critical and more patient, to reward small signs of progress, and to set people up to succeed."

Today, visitors of all sorts, from all over the world, come to our ranch to learn about leadership, trust, teamwork, and communication. Some of their stories are contained in these pages, as are the stories of many horses I've had the privilege of knowing (in some instances, names have been changed to protect privacy). At the end of the day, I'm a horse trainer, not a management consultant, and I'm certainly not a therapist. I've often wondered what qualifies me—a cowboy with barely a high school education—to be teaching these accomplished leaders anything. The truth is, it's the horses who do the teaching—I just try to translate.

At one point, when I was thinking about this unexpected path my life has taken, I opened my Bible to read the phrase "Son of man, set forth an allegory."* That spoke to me immediately. I believe the horses do provide something akin to an allegory. When people watch me working with a horse, or read the stories about the horses I've trained, they are able to interpret what they witness and uncover truths there that are meaningful in their lives. They find themselves reflecting on their own faults or mistakes, recognizing their potential to be better, and maybe even admitting to fears and wounds they'd previously kept hidden. The lessons they take away help them to be more effective leaders in their workplaces and better parents to their kids. For some, they help with overcoming trauma or addiction, forgiving

---

* Ezekiel 17:2.

estranged loved ones, confronting fears, building confidence, or finding their passion in life.

In the decades I've been doing this work, I've seen over and over how it changes people—and always for the good. I've seen tough and insensitive people become softer and more empathetic. I've seen timid and fearful people become firmer and more confident. I've seen proud and arrogant people become humble and vulnerable. None of these changes happened because I told people what was wrong with them. They simply saw themselves reflected in the mirror of the horse and started working on it.

For every lesson I've shared with the people who come to the ranch, there's a lesson *I've* learned as well. It's been my privilege to work with some of the great leaders in business and politics, and I take away many nuggets of wisdom from our conversations, our correspondence, and from simply observing them as they interact with their teams at the ranch. I've been struck, again and again, by the similarities in the ways they lead their companies and the principles I learned for training horses. The principles I share in the pages of this book are informed by the examples of all the great leaders I know, both two- and four-legged.

A Sermon You Can See

If you're wondering about the wisdom of applying horse-training methods to human beings, let me be clear: people are not the same as horses, and what works with horses doesn't always work with people. Moreover, what I'm sharing is not a method but a philosophy. It's a set of guiding principles for forming healthier relationships—with horses, with people, and with ourselves. Every horse is different, like every human being, so what works for one individual in one moment might not work for another in a different moment. If you reduce "thinking like a horse" to a method, which many people do, it will quickly become fixed and limiting. But if you can grasp the philosophy at its core, and keep coming back to it, it will guide you to the right solutions for whatever situation you happen to be in.

Before we get started, I'd like to share a poem. I love the tradition of cowboy poetry. At the end of a demonstration, I often climb on an upturned bucket beside the horse, leaning over his back to get him used to having me up above him—preparation for when I'll actually sit up there in the saddle. As he starts to relax, I'll sometimes stay up on that bucket, a hand resting on the horse's neck, and recite verses to our guests. Later, around the campfire, they often ask for more. One of my favorite poems—that becomes a favorite of many of the leaders I work with—was written more than a hundred years ago by Edgar A. Guest. It's called "Sermons We See" and it goes like this:

I'd rather see a sermon than hear one any day;
I'd rather one should walk with me than merely tell the way.
The eye's a better pupil and more willing than the ear,
Fine counsel is confusing, but example's always clear;
And the best of all the preachers are the men who live their
creeds,

All I Really Need to Know I Learned from a Horse

For to see good put in action is what everybody needs.
I soon can learn to do it if you'll let me see it done;
I can watch your hands in action, but your tongue too fast
may run.
And the lecture you deliver may be very wise and true,
But I'd rather get my lessons by observing what you do;
For I might misunderstand you and the high advice you give,
But there's no misunderstanding how you act and how you live.
When I see a deed of kindness, I am eager to be kind.
When a weaker brother stumbles and a strong man stays behind
Just to see if he can help him, then the wish grows strong in me
To become as big and thoughtful as I know that friend to be.
And all travelers can witness that the best of guides today
Is not the one who tells them, but the one who shows the way.
One good man teaches many, men believe what they behold;
One deed of kindness noticed is worth forty that are told.
Who stands with men of honor learns to hold his honor dear,
For right living speaks a language which to every one is clear.
Though an able speaker charms me with his eloquence, I say,
I'd rather see a sermon than to hear one, any day.*

As I invite you into these pages to meet the people and the horses I have known, my wish is that through my words, you will "see" the events I'm describing. I have no wish to preach to

---

* Edgar A. Guest, "Sermons We See," *Collected Verse of Edgar A. Guest* (Chicago: Riley & Lee, 1943), 599. First published in *The Boy Agriculturist*, vols. 12–13, Illinois State Training School for Boys, 1919.

you. But I witness small miracles every day in my round pen and in the lives of the people who gather around the fence. The horses have taught me so much about how to be a better father, a better husband, a better leader, and a better human being.

I hope that in their stories, you, too, can see the sermon they are sharing.

CHAPTER ONE

You Can't Lie to a Horse

No philosophers so thoroughly
comprehend us as dogs and horses.
They see through us at a glance.

—HERMAN MELVILLE

THE GALLOPING HOOFBEATS slowed and came to a halt. The frightened young horse had stopped running around the pen and turned toward the middle, where I stood. I could hear his heavy breathing and smell the sweat that streaked his rich chestnut coat—the inspiration for the name we'd given him, Wildfire. Not long ago, he'd been living wild with a herd of mustangs, never touched by a human hand. Now it was up to me to teach him how to live and work with people so that he could be adopted into a good home.

"He's considering that maybe I'm not so scary after all," I told the group of people watching from the fence. "I can't force him to trust me; he has to decide to do that for himself. I want him to choose to face his fear, rather than fleeing. So what I'm doing is making the right thing easy and the wrong thing difficult. Running away is hard work. Coming to be with me is easy. He can rest here in the middle."

The horse hadn't quite realized this yet, but I noted that his expression had changed. His wild eyes were softening, and he was lowering his head, a sign of submission. Soon, I could tell, he'd be ready to walk slowly toward me, and I'd feel his warm breath as he reached out his head to sniff me. I knelt down in the dirt, making myself as small and unthreatening as possible. He'd shown respect to me, so now it was time for me to show humility to him, to release the pressure and indicate that I was not a predator.

As I waited for the colt to take those first tentative steps of trust, something on the other side of the pen caught my attention. Standing by the fence was a young cowboy, tears streaming down his handsome face.

Jeremy Morris was our first employee at Diamond Cross Ranch, and at that point he'd been working for us for just a couple of weeks—or rather, as my wife, Jane, and I liked to joke, *we'd* been working for *him*. A born leader with natural confidence and charisma, Jeremy was the kind of guy people loved to be around and were quick to follow. But he didn't take direction easily. Not long after he began working for us, I asked him to ride a horse I'd recently gotten in a trade.

"Don't tie him up tight," I warned. I'd already learned that this triggered panic in the horse. He would pull back violently, fighting the rope and risking injury to himself and anyone around him. But Jeremy didn't listen, and that horse freaked out. He reared up, breaking the rope, and then flipped over backward, scuffing up Jeremy's saddle. Luckily no one was hurt, but they could have been.

Jeremy was good at his job, but he'd always push the boundaries. He'd show up tired for work because he'd been out partying the night before. Still, he was talented with the horses and cows (and great with our corporate clients, who thought he looked like a Western movie star in his buckaroo outfit and silk bandana). The other ranch hands liked him, and our kids adored him. So we tried to make it work. Jane and I were inexperienced leaders ourselves at that time, so I'm sure we made our share of mistakes.

Jeremy had been around horses his whole life and had come to us because he wanted to learn my training methods. Like me, he'd been raised with the tough cowboy approach, but he was intrigued by the possibility of a way to train horses that didn't rely on fear, pain, or force. I'd explained to him that I couldn't really teach him a method, but I could share the philosophy—the set of principles that all my training is based on. Every horse is different, and each one requires a somewhat different approach, but the principles stay consistent.

I know these principles—which I'll be sharing in the pages ahead—work with horses. I've seen it hundreds, if not thousands, of times. But back in those days, I had only a hunch that they might apply to humans as well. So it surprised me to see the impact of my words and my demonstration on the young cowboy by the ringside.

Today, almost two decades later, I wouldn't be surprised at

all. It's become common for people to approach me after demonstrations with tears in their eyes. I've seen powerful CEOs grapple with their own shortcomings as leaders while watching a wild horse respond to firm but gentle boundaries. I've seen fathers break down in tears, recognizing that they were too harsh with their children. I've seen grown men and women begin to release decades of hidden trauma as they understand for the first time that it's safe to trust. I've learned that the horses have an extraordinary ability to reveal people to themselves. In so doing, they become a powerful catalyst for personal growth and leadership development.

Like I often say: you can lie to others, and you can lie to yourself, but you can't lie to a horse.

A Horse Is Like a Mirror

Why is it that so many of us can be truly ourselves around a horse? Perhaps it's because horses see us for who we really are. As prey animals, they're highly sensitive, attuned to human body language and energy. Horses have a direct line of sight to what's inside of us. They see who we really are, not who we pretend to be. They intuitively know what we're made of, and they can sense our intentions.

"Put a wild horse in the middle of a group of people, and it will pick out the most dangerous guy, every time," says my friend Mike Buchanan. Mike worked at the nearby Honor

Farm, running a program that taught ex-convicts to gentle and train mustangs. It's a win-win idea: these men, who are getting ready to reenter society, get to learn some valuable skills, and the horses get trained so they can be put up for public adoption. Mike said that when a new group arrived, he would tell the guys to stand around the edge of a big pen, and then he would turn a horse loose inside. That horse would run around, and pretty soon it would throw its head up and snort at a particular fellow in the group. Without fail, the horse knew which among the men was the most dangerous criminal. The horse could also pick out the *least* threatening guy—the one at the bottom of the pecking order—and would be drawn to him.

Sometimes a horse knows us even better than we know ourselves.

A favorite poem of mine is called "The Guy in the Glass" by Peter Dale Wimbrow Sr. It's about the idea that we all have to answer to ourselves in the end—"The feller whose verdict counts most in your life / Is the guy staring back from the glass."* Oftentimes, for this very reason, we avoid taking a good hard look in the mirror. We're embarrassed, ashamed, or just not brave enough to reckon with who we are.

This is where I'm grateful for the horses in my life. They've acted as a mirror, reflecting my own shortcomings back to me even when I didn't want to see them. They've helped me to see myself as I am, not as who I hope to be or pretend to be.

---

* Peter Dale Wimbrow Sr., "The Guy in the Glass," originally published in *The American Magazine*, 1934.

Too many of us hide from ourselves, pushing the parts we don't like out of sight and going about our business, hoping others won't see them. But if you're walking through life trying to look like someone you're not, that's hard work. You can't keep it up for too long. You build up shame and self-hatred around the things you're hiding, and you live in fear of them leaking out for all the world to see.

Many people find it hard to admit their own faults, weaknesses, vulnerabilities, wounds, or fears—even to themselves. For someone in a leadership position, whom people look up to, this can be doubly true. And yet it's critical that we find a way to be honest about all of who we are. If we are to grow, as leaders, as parents, and as human beings, and be able to help others do the same, we need to stop pretending. I think that's why so many people find the experience at our ranch to be life-changing. No one's pointing out their faults or confronting them with their fears, but they naturally start being more real with themselves. It's a safe place to see themselves honestly—and to see the possibility of transformation.

We Live What We've Learned

For Wildfire, like hundreds of other horses I've known over the years, I was his last chance. He'd been adopted by well-meaning but inexperienced folks who loved the romantic idea of owning a mustang but hadn't the first idea what to do with a wild horse. He'd ended up in their backyard, and they couldn't even get close to him. After a few failed attempts and a couple of close calls, he'd been written off as "dangerous" and "untrainable."

"That horse is more trouble than he's worth," I'd been told. As I began to work with him, it wasn't hard to see why. At first, he galloped wildly around the pen, clearly terrified of human contact. I just waved the long-handled flag I carried, encouraging him to run. I didn't blame him for his behavior. Who knew what he'd been through in his short life. Had he been terrorized by helicopter roundups and loud-voiced men who tore him away from his herd? Had he been trapped in a narrow chute, branded, vaccinated, and packed into a dark, noisy truck with other frightened colts? As I told Jeremy and the others watching that day, "He's just living what he's learned."

Every horse that comes to me is living what he's learned. He has a story, but he can't tell it. If I don't know his story—and I often don't—all I have to go on are the signs he gives me. Pay close enough attention and it's not hard to connect the dots. Certain triggers will provoke certain reactions. A horse that's head-shy—afraid of having his face or ears touched and being haltered—may have been beaten. A horse that's aggressive may have been spoiled, allowed to get away with disrespectful behavior until he's become dangerous. Humans traumatize horses in countless ways—sometimes out of cruelty, but more often simply out of ignorance. Many people don't realize there is a better way.

Sometimes you need a lot of patience to see the good in a horse when the fears from his past are overshadowing his strengths.

"You gotta believe in him and treat him like the horse you know he can be, not the horse he's being right now," I told Jeremy and the others. "It's not just about today; it's about the rest of his life. If you only focus on what he's doing wrong, you won't have the patience to help him grow into his potential." I always say, if you don't believe in a horse—or a person, for that matter—you shouldn't be working with him in the first place.

Over the course of an hour or so, Jeremy watched as I drove the colt in circles—letting him run, giving him the freedom to move his feet. Horses are flight animals, and they're naturally claustrophobic. If you trap them, they'll panic and fight. But if you let a horse run, he'll gain confidence. I don't hobble horses or tie them down in the way the old horse-breakers did. With enough rope, you can restrain a horse, but that won't make him trust you. It just drives the fear inside. Like the great horsemen I learned from, I do almost all of my initial work with horses in a round pen, without restraints. The round pen has no corners where a horse can get trapped, so despite the fact that it's a small space, it allows them to keep moving. They always have an escape route. A round pen has soft footing and solid fencing, so they can't hurt themselves. This makes it a perfect environment for training because the horse feels relatively safe.

I want horses to feel like they have the freedom to choose. I respect their intelligence and their instincts. I keep my body language as nonthreatening as possible, and I let them keep running until they make the decision to turn toward me and face their fear on their own terms. Horses appreciate being given this freedom.

I think human beings are very much the same. We don't want someone telling us what to do and forcing us against our will. We're much more likely to trust and learn from others when we're allowed the freedom to make our own choices. That's what Wildfire did. Panic slowly gave way to curiosity, until the young horse chose, of his own accord, to approach me, head lowered as a sign of submission.

There are few moments in life that are more magical than those when a wild animal freely decides to give you his trust. As I reached out to touch him and let him sniff me, I felt the sense of wonder I always feel at that first moment of connection, which some horse trainers call "hooking on" or "joining up." But in this particular instance, my mind was also on the cowboy. What was Jeremy seeing as he watched the horse? What had moved him to tears?

What story was *he* carrying inside?

———

Unlocking Hope

It wasn't the moment to ask, that much I knew. People are like horses in this regard: you can't force them to trust you, or corner them and expect that they'll open up. All you can do is create an environment in which they feel safe, be patient and consistent, and give them the freedom to choose. Trust is the essential foundation of any relationship, whether with a human or an animal. And it doesn't come easily to most of us. That can be hard when you care about someone. "Why won't my teenager talk to me?" "Why didn't my partner share what's really going on?" "Why don't my employees tell me what they actually think?" The answer? They haven't yet decided it's safe to do so.

When Jeremy worked for us, it was clear he didn't have the words to speak about what had happened in his life, any more than the mustang colt did. But I sensed that it had been hard— much harder than anything I'd personally experienced. Eventually, he moved on to work for a neighboring ranch, but we remained close. It would be many, many years before I would learn what was behind those tears.

"I didn't have the language or the bravery to tell anyone my story," he confirmed later. "I didn't even admit it to myself. I didn't know the pain I was in." The only clues to his troubled past were a certain look he'd get in his eyes—a combination of fear and anger, not dissimilar to the eyes of a wild and frightened horse—and a set of self-destructive behaviors that I had come to know all too well over the two summers he worked for us and in the years that followed.

Jeremy had spent his whole life trying to stay ahead of his past, fleeing his inner demons. When he felt cornered and couldn't outrun them, he'd try to drink them into submission instead. He lived in our bunkhouse, and we loved him like family. People were drawn to him wherever he went, but perhaps that only drove his secrets deeper inside—as if he were afraid that people wouldn't like him if they knew the truth.

"Secrets can kill you," Jeremy says today. "They almost killed me." He means that literally. After he stopped working for us, he bounced around a lot, met and married a wonderful girl named Mary, became a father, and almost lost all of it when his secret drinking and compulsive lies drove a wedge into his marriage. Life gave him chance after chance—several dream jobs, talent to burn, and a wife and friends who loved him—but none of those things could free him from the destructive effects of his self-hatred.

"There was this pit of pain deep inside me," he says.

For years, his buried story ate away at him, robbing him of sleep, of peace, and of any ability to trust, particularly when it came to women. Eventually, separated from his wife and baby son, he reached a point where he was drinking a bottle of whiskey a night, all by himself. He drove blackout drunk from Arizona to Wyoming pulling a trailer full of horses. When he woke up in a truck stop, missing a mirror, he had no memory of how he'd gotten there. But even that didn't stop him. The next day, after dropping off the horses, he was pulled over and given a DUI—his fourth. He kept drinking as he drove back to Jackson, Wyoming.

"I'd reached a point where it felt like life wasn't worth living anymore. I considered just driving off the road," he recalls. And then, as he was heading up Teton Pass, he heard a siren behind him. His fifth DUI, the second in forty-eight hours. And in

Wyoming, this meant going straight to jail and staying there until you see a judge. Jeremy had no choice but to stop running.

That night, standing in the corner of a crowded holding cell with more than a dozen other men, he felt utter despair. He was in so much trouble. Five DUIs. How was he going to tell his wife? There was no way his fragile marriage could survive this. He was broke, and now there would be legal fees and fines to pay. He might face jail time. And he didn't know if he had what it would take to beat his addiction. He'd tried so much already—gone to the meetings, counted the days, done the counseling.

"It just wasn't in me," he says. During that long sleepless night, he had nothing left to do but pray. And a question arose in his heart: "If I could be free of this addiction, what kind of father could I be?" He accepted that his marriage might be over, but he felt a sudden, acute longing to be there for his son, Layton, in a way that his own parents had never been for him.

The story Jeremy had never told, even to himself, began when he was six years old. His parents divorced, taking one child each, and Jeremy was left with his deeply depressed father and a string of stepmothers, one of whom physically and emotionally abused him for years, while his father remained oblivious. "I'd go to school with scratches and bruises," he remembers. But that wasn't all. As a boy, he was repeatedly sexually molested; first by an older boy, later by a babysitter and a female family member. Too young to really understand what was happening, he never spoke about it. "I knew it was wrong," he says, "but I was too ashamed to tell anyone." The thought of his churchgoing grandparents finding out what had happened filled him with horror.

"I blamed myself. . . . I started asking, 'What have I done to deserve this?' There was no way I could say anything to anyone." He buried it so deep that he didn't even remember it, except in moments when something cracked through—a letter from his mother, a picture of his first abuser popping up on Facebook, having too much to drink—and he'd blurt out something to a friend or to his wife. But then, just as quickly, he'd shut down again, refusing to say another word.

When I asked him, years later, what moved him to tears that day watching me with Wildfire at the ranch, he said, "It was the way you didn't get offended by horses' mistakes and bad behavior. You could see the good in every horse, and you didn't judge them for the way they acted out—even the wild and crazy ones. You understood that they'd been hurt. That touched me."

He paused, as if replaying the scene in his mind. "Somewhere, I knew that the poor choices and mistakes I kept making were driven by my past. But because I couldn't look at my past, I just kept judging myself and hating myself. Watching you work with that horse was one of the moments when I saw the possibility of a different life. You were unlocking hope. I wouldn't find my own way for many years, but I knew that you saw the good in me, too. You never gave up on me, even when I was close to giving up on myself."

That night in the Wyoming jail, Jeremy had never been closer to giving up. "I can only describe what happened next as grace," he says. "I just knew, all of a sudden, I was never going to drink again. It left me. I felt hope for the first time ever. That DUI saved my life." He's been sober now for more than a decade, and he and Mary have three sons. It's been a long road, but he finally found a way to tell his story—first to himself, then to his family and friends, to counselors, and more recently, in public forums. It's still coming back to him, emerging out of the dark recesses where he buried those painful memories. He's become passionate about helping other men find the courage to open up about abuse—something he's been surprised to learn is far more prevalent among men than he realized.

Today, Jeremy has become the leader he always seemed born to be. He's built a thriving business. When working with his employees, he often recalls the lessons he learned from the horses, and from his own journey.

"Honestly," he says, "as a CEO, I think I spend eighty percent of my time on my people's emotional health or on helping them deal with friction between them. When someone responds negatively in a work situation, I've learned not to react but to ask, Why? I know they each have a story, but they may not be able to tell it. They're living what they've learned."

Strong Fences; Soft Footing

When I finally heard Jeremy's story just a few years ago, I remembered him standing by the round pen watching the mustang a decade earlier, crying tears that even he didn't understand.

Back then, as his boss, I didn't know how to help him—and he wouldn't have been ready to receive help even if I'd been able to give it. I had to let him move on and find his own way, and the road ahead of him was a long and hard one.

Today, I know more about people, and I appreciate that we've all been hurt—physically, emotionally, or mentally. Perhaps not as severely as Jeremy, but the scars are there nonetheless. And if we're not willing to face our fears and tell our stories, they'll trip us up again and again. I've heard it said that hidden emotions never die, and I believe that to be true—with people and with horses. When it comes to horses, if you ignore the signs, eventually those emotions will reveal themselves under pressure. When you're trying to rope a sick calf, or gather the herd before a storm—those times when you most need the horse to be reliable—he'll quit you.

Jeremy's pain was deep, and the ways in which he acted out were correspondingly extreme. For others, the triggers might be more subtle and the behaviors less dramatic. But they will sabotage higher potential. Most people know what it's like to have a friend, colleague, partner, or family member who is oversensitive to the slightest criticism. Most leaders know what it's like to have an employee who repeatedly makes the same mistakes and undermines their own progress. Most teachers know what it's like to have a student who turns every lesson into a battle. They're living what they've learned.

If we're too quick to judge someone for their behavior, we close the door to change. That doesn't mean we have to just accept behavior that is destructive. The round pen in which I train the horses has strong fences. But it also has soft footing. As leaders or parents, we are always creating environments for the people we work with or live with. Those environments are not made of posts and rails; they are made of our own attitudes. Clear boundaries, patience, humility, transparency, slowness to judge, and compassion for the wounds we cannot see: these are the pillars of the safe space we can build.

While no human being is perfect, we can all learn to be better—better parents, leaders, partners, friends, mentors, or coaches. We can learn to inspire trust and authenticity in others. And the lessons the horses teach us can help. We can remember that every person is living what they've learned. We can be patient and resist the urge to judge based on appearances. We can tell ourselves: it's not just about today; it's about the rest of their lives.

We can each create a space in which other people feel safe to stop running.

CHAPTER TWO

Feel Can't Be Taught, but It Can Be Learned

*The most important thing in communication
is hearing what isn't said.*

—PETER F. DRUCKER

D O YOU FEEL THAT?"
I used to get asked this question many times a day by Tink Elordi, a great horseman I began to work with and learn from back in the late eighties.

"Lift up on one rein," he'd suggest. Or, "Hang in there. Wait for him to turn loose." He'd watch intently to see how the horse responded. Then he'd say, "*There.* Do you feel that?"

Sometimes I did—I'd sense the horse relaxing or softening. But more often, back in those days, I didn't really know what Tink was getting at. The horse felt just about the same to me, and usually it wasn't doing what I wanted it to do. Frustrated, I'd shake my head.

It was embarrassing. I'd been working with horses my whole life, and now, at the age of thirty, I hated feeling like a beginner again. But I knew I needed to be honest with Tink if I wanted to become the kind of trainer he was—one who worked with his horses rather than against them. And I really wanted that. Besides, I was paying him a lot of my hard-earned money.

Over the few years prior, I'd been slowly growing dissatisfied with myself. Training horses for polo, and playing the game myself, I'd achieved some success, but I'd also seen the costs. Selling horses was necessary in my business, yet I often felt as if I were betraying them. Sometimes, horses I'd sold would get ruined or injured by poor riders. More than once, tempted by a much-needed payday, I sold a horse before it was ready and then watched all my work be undone. And the pressure to train and sell horses quickly in order to turn a profit led me to use forceful methods to get the animals to conform. I'd always had a natural way with difficult horses and been good at getting them to do what I wanted. But sometimes in those days, I felt like I was working *against* my horses rather than with them. I often became so discouraged I was tempted to give it up completely and find another career. That's when I began to search.

The unexpected answer to my prayers came when my boss took me to a horse-training clinic held by famed horseman Ray Hunt. I'd tried to read Ray's iconic book, *Think Harmony with Horses,* almost a decade before, but back then I didn't even get through it, not grasping what he was trying to say.

Seeing Ray work in person was captivating. He removed the horse's bridle and declared: "If you can direct his mind, his feet will follow." As he was speaking, the horse would turn his head left and then right, without any visible guidance from the man on his back. Ray explained that he was creating harmony with the horse by listening, paying attention to subtle signals, and respecting the horse's intelligence. And he summed all that up in one simple word: *feel.*

How to "Have Feel"

Feel. That's what Tink was getting at when he asked me, "Do you feel that?" I'd sought out Tink after meeting Ray, because I knew I needed a teacher if I were to learn how to apply this new philosophy of horse training. Tink was known as one of the best colt starters in the business, and he had worked with both Ray and Ray's mentor Tom Dorrance. A big, intimidating man with a black belt in karate, Tink had a gruff manner. But when he got on a horse, he rode with surprising grace and lightness.

"Search for that softness," he'd always tell me. Being soft didn't mean he was holding the reins with his fingertips—it meant he was sensitive but ready to be firm if needed.

Tink explained that feel is not just something you do; it's something you can *have,* and something you need to develop. If you "have feel" it means you're in tune with how a horse is feeling and how she might react, reading her body language and responding in ways that build her trust and confidence. Great horsemen and -women have developed feel.

Feel is a combination of sensitivity, intuition, and empathy. It's one of the most important things to learn when working with horses or with people. If I could teach you one thing in these pages, it would be feel. But feel can't really be taught; it can only be learned. You have to develop it through tuning in, observing, paying attention, experimenting, listening, and trying to put yourself inside the experience of another.

Tink knew that, which is why he just patiently kept asking the question—*Can you feel that?*—and setting up scenarios so I could learn through practice.

This use of the term "feel" might not be common outside the field of horsemanship, but it points to something everyone has experienced. We've all run into people who just seem naturally attuned to others. They appear to sense how people are feeling and intuitively know the right way to respond. They're not lost in their own heads or caught up in their own agendas. And we've all met the opposite as well: people who are insensitive, blind to the impact they're having, and careless in their responses. They act as if their own feelings are all that matter, or they assume that other people feel just like they do. That's feel—or the lack of it.

People in business might use terms like "emotional intelligence," but it comes down to the same thing. Great leaders have it, but they sometimes can't put it into words. Well-meaning consultants and human resources folks try to teach it, but it's not something that can be easily reduced to a set of skills or behaviors. Once again, feel can't be taught—but it can be developed, if we have a little patience and humility and are willing to work at it.

Not long ago, I was chatting about feel with a wonderful leader and horseman named Dave Balzhiser. Dave spent his career at the building materials supplier Simpson Strong-Tie, working his way up from the factory floor to vice president, as the company grew from a small business to a billion-dollar public company. Dave and I had met years ago at a horse show in Elko, Nevada. We struck up a conversation late one night while working our horses in the practice ring. It turned out to be the first of many deep discussions about how horses can help improve our leadership. On the topic of feel, Dave came up with a great analogy:

"I always ask people, do you remember the first time you drove a manual or stick-shift car? Your driving instructor probably told you, 'Here's first gear, here's second, here's third, here's fourth, and over and down is reverse.' They showed you the clutch on the left, the brake in the middle, and the gas on the right and explained how you drive. But no matter how well they described it, what's the first thing that happens when you try it? You stall. . . . And the only way to learn is to just keep doing it, until you get to the point where it's second nature. You can sense exactly that point where you need to release the brake, ease off the clutch, and press the accelerator, to find the right gear. *That's* what feel is like. No amount of explaining can really teach you how to do it. You have to learn for yourself."

Here's the thing about learning: it's uncomfortable. It's one thing when you're a kid in school; it's another thing altogether when you're an adult who's supposed to have life figured out, let alone a parent who's raising kids of your own. And if you're looked up to as a leader or an expert, the last thing you want to do is let on that you have something to learn. That's how I sometimes felt in those sessions with Tink. And I observe the same thing in some of the leaders I work with. They're afraid to admit that they struggle to understand their employees or feel clumsy when dealing with people. They think that acknowledging their own faults or shortcomings will disqualify them from being a leader. Actually, the opposite is true. Leaders who are transparent put people at ease and make them feel safe.

Part of learning feel—though not all of it—is reading body language. Because animals don't speak English, the main way they communicate is nonverbal. If you have a pet dog or cat, you probably have some skill at reading this kind of communication already. Gracie, our border collie, is very clear. She tells us with her eyes when she's excited and ready to go chase cows. And when she doesn't feel like going out, she drops her head down low.

Horses give us all kinds of cues in this way, too. Sometimes they're obvious, like a narrowed angry eye or pinned ears. Other times, they're more subtle, like the licking of lips that signifies relief, or a certain softening in the eyes. People communicate this way, too, but often we don't have the eyes to see it. Horses are much easier to read than humans—and they're better at reading *our* body language as well.

When I introduce myself to a horse that has been put in the round pen, the first thing I do is simply move about the pen, allowing the horse to move freely around me. My body language is completely relaxed and nonthreatening. I don't glare at the horse with my eyes or face him head-on. I turn my shoulders slightly away, showing him that I am not confronting him in any way. I like to walk around him, allowing him the freedom to flee, without pursuing him as a predator would. This helps the horse realize he is not being attacked, and he will soon become comfortable in his new surroundings.

A horse in the wild is always on high alert. As a prey animal, she has to be ready to flee at any moment, so she's intensely attuned to her surroundings—to the movements of others in the herd, the smells on the breeze, the rustling in the bushes. She may appear relaxed, grazing on the lush green grass and enjoying the sunshine on her back, but she's always aware. That's what it means to be prey. Some people contrast this with the consciousness of humans, who are predators. But I don't think it's quite that simple. Humans can certainly be predators, but we know how it feels to be prey as well. When we feel threatened, we can develop that kind of alertness we see in the wild horse.

As a child, I developed an unusual sensitivity to the people around me, and I think much of it resulted from my desire to avoid criticism or anger from my father. I learned how to read every nuance of his body language. I'd do anything to avoid conflict—a trait that stayed with me long after I grew up and left home, and long after my dad mellowed out and became much less critical. I got very good at getting people on my side and defusing situations.

Of course, that's not always the best approach, but I do think it helped me when it came to the horses. My skills of observation and empathy were already quite well-developed, and I didn't want to fight with horses any more than I wanted to fight with my dad. Being around so many tough cowboys and polo players, who were all about force and fear, I lost touch with some of my sensitivity. But it was still who I was underneath. That's why I was attracted to the gentler methods of horsemen like Ray Hunt, Tink Elordi, and Tom Dorrance—they reawakened my natural "feel" and gave me words to describe it and a philosophy to develop it.

Under Tink's tutorship, I began having conversations with my horses again. Above all, I was listening to them—paying attention for the signs that would tell me how they were feeling. I learned how to lead a colt and sense when he was about to pull back on the rope. Rather than holding him up tight, right under his chin, in anticipation of a battle, I could give him some freedom but stay sensitive to his signals. When I felt him about to resist, I could change angles and soften my grip before he did so, keeping him soft and moving forward in harmony with me. I discovered that when the horse's mind is right, a thousand-pound animal can be light as a feather, able to be directed with a finger.

Ray used to say that before a horse does anything—bucking, kicking, biting, spooking—he gets ready to do it. As you get more experienced around horses (and other creatures), you learn to read those signs and head off the unwanted behavior before it happens. If you're surprised by something a horse does, that just means you probably weren't listening carefully enough to what he was telling you in the moment right before.

I often think about this principle in relationship to people. How many bad things that happen in the world could be averted if we were paying more attention to the unspoken messages of those around us? When I see a tragedy on the news, like a kid shooting up a school or a guy going on an armed rampage, I often wonder, What were the signs that were missed? Could this have been prevented if the people around had more empathy, better feel, and of course, the willingness to help that person? And am I paying enough attention to those around me? What are they telling *me* without words?

Pressure and Release

These days, when folks visit the ranch, I'm paying attention to their body language and unconscious cues in the same way I pay attention to the horses. A few years back, a photographer named John Balsom came to take photos at the ranch. He brought his wife and young son, and they stayed in our home for a couple of weeks. John has won numerous awards for capturing the way he sees the world, but it was the eyes behind the camera that captured my attention. There was a certain look he'd get as he lowered his lens—a sadness, even a hint of bitterness, that seemed at odds with everything else about this friendly and accomplished young Englishman. His wiry frame was a little stooped around a back injury, but I could tell the pain was deeper than physical. Earlier in my life, I might have missed it completely or dismissed it out of hand. But after decades of studying horses and people, I sometimes find myself unable to turn away when I perceive an unspoken message. What were his eyes telling me? I wondered. I didn't want to pry. But I also sensed he'd ended up here for a reason, and it wasn't just to photograph the horses or the breathtaking views.

One day, John was shooting by the round pen as I saddled a skittish young gray mare named Ghost for the first time. Ghost had had a rough start in life, and it had taken several sessions to gain her trust. She stood still as I threw the saddle blanket over her a few times, rubbing it up and down, getting her accustomed to having something on her back.

"It's okay, girl, it's not a lion," I told her, leaning my weight over the blanket. Her head was high, her nervous system on alert, but she didn't buck or bolt. "Good girl." I ran my hand along her neck and praised her. When the time came to place the heavy leather saddle on her back, she stood calmly. I tightened the cinch and encouraged her to walk forward.

After I'd worked her in the saddle for a while, I told John, "I think she's ready for a rider."

"How do you know?" he asked.

I thought about the question for a moment. I didn't really know—you can't always tell for sure that it's safe to get on a horse's back for the first time. That's why many of the old horsebreakers used to rope the horse and tie up one of its legs, forcing it to stand still and be mounted. But since I don't use ropes or restraints in that way, I rely on feel. I have to tune in to what the horse is feeling, what her body language tells me, what her energy is signaling. Does she trust me enough to allow me to do something that goes against her survival instincts? Is she relaxed and paying attention to me, or is she tense and likely to panic? Is she telling me that she's had painful or frightening experiences in the past when people tried to ride her, or is this just new and unfamiliar? Does she want to please, or is she resisting the process? Have I already done enough for today or is she open to more?

My intuition about Ghost was that she trusted me, and she wasn't aggressive or overly fearful. She'd made important steps forward already, but her positive energy and alertness encouraged me to ask her for one more step. I was proved right. She allowed me to ease my weight into the saddle and walked tentatively forward without bucking. John's camera, and his troubled eyes, followed our slow progress around the pen.

I kept that first ride short, wanting to be sure to end on a good note. That's an important part of feel as well—knowing when to stop and when to reward progress. If you have good feel, you'll sense the small changes and know that they represent the horse trying. No, she's not perfect and the change may not be dramatic. But it's a change, and that's what matters. One brick in her foundation—something to build on.

After I'd dismounted and praised the gray mare, I asked John, "What do you see?" What I really wanted to know was what he was feeling, but I didn't know him well enough to ask that question yet.

John was quiet for a moment, watching the horse as she rested her forehead against my shoulder and blew a big sigh through her velvety-soft nose. "Repair," he said. "These horses are experiencing repair. It's like you're helping to rebuild bridges between horses and humans."

As John's visit drew to an end, I wrestled with myself. Should I ask him about himself? Or should I just keep my mouth shut? I was reluctant to overstep, but I had a sense he was here for more than a few photographs. I decided to risk asking him more directly about what in his own life might need repair.

"I see a sadness in your eyes," I told him. "Is there some kind of pain or hurt from your past that might need to be healed or forgiven?"

He seemed surprised at my question, but like the mare, he trusted me enough to tentatively step forward without recoiling.

"I didn't have a bad childhood," he said. "We had a comfortable middle-class life, and I didn't want for anything. But I am still angry at my dad, who walked out when I was just seven. I'm not mad that he left. I get it—some marriages don't work out. But I can't get my head around how he could abandon all responsibility for us and not even pay a penny toward supporting his children."

I asked John if he'd been in touch with his father recently, but he said it had been a while. "I haven't even told him he's a grandfather," he said. "And my son is now six years old."

During John's stay at the ranch, I shared what I understood about the power of forgiveness, and even invited a friend to tell his own powerful story of forgiving the father who had abused him as a child. I could sense that John was taking it in, but he still wasn't sure what he would choose to do with it. He seemed like a naturally reserved kind of guy, and none of this had been on his agenda when he showed up to take photos and get away from the big city for a few days. So I backed off a bit and didn't push. People, like horses, don't generally respond well to constant pressure. Leading with feel involves a dance of pressure and release. If you don't release, you don't allow space for learning and response.

About a week after John's visit, I received a message from him thanking me for our conversations. He told me that the day he'd left, he'd called his dad from the airport—the first time they'd spoken in many years—and told him that he was a grandfather. The very next day, when John arrived home in London, his dad came to visit.

"Have I totally forgiven him for what he did?" John reflects. "No. But I didn't want to deprive my son of a grandfather just because I was deprived of a father. When I watched them together, throwing paper planes in the park, I realized I didn't need to bring up all that stuff from the past. It just wasn't the right moment. So I let it go. I've moved on. And I don't think that would have happened if I hadn't visited the ranch. I was too stubborn and bitter."

Hearing John's story made me appreciate once again the power of trusting one's intuition. All I did was pay attention to what I saw in his eyes. I didn't know all that it meant, but I had a sense that it was worth pursuing. And because his heart had been touched by what he saw with the horses, he was willing to open up. As a result, the lives of three generations were changed.

Trying to Feel

It doesn't take any special skill or qualification to pay attention and lead with feel. But it does take humility and the willingness to learn. We human beings tend to be easily distracted by the busyness of the world around us, or we become absorbed in our own thoughts and feelings. We miss the cues that are in front of our eyes. Or we see them but interpret them wrongly because we're looking through the filter of our own feelings. It takes discipline and care to tune in to other people and give them enough of our attention that we can sense what's going on beneath the surface.

Feel isn't something you just learn once and then you have it. You keep working at it. That's what I hope you'll be doing as you read through this book. I hope that you'll be putting this philosophy into practice, paying close attention to the results, and asking yourself: "Did I feel that?" It's okay if your answer isn't always "Yes."

What matters is that you are trying.

CHAPTER THREE

Give Him the Name You Want Him to Live Up To

"Sometimes I think you believe in me
more than I do," said the boy.
"You'll catch up," said the horse.

—CHARLIE MACKESY,
The Boy, the Mole, the Fox and the Horse

THE BLACK HORSE STOOD almost six feet high at the shoulder and weighed about fifteen hundred pounds. His coat was the color of gleaming coal, and his face was marked by a bold white blaze that stood out between his wary eyes. Imagine one of the Budweiser horses crossed with a racehorse and you'll get a pretty good sense of how he looked. His sheer bulk made him intimidating, but in fact he was one of the most terrified creatures I've ever met.

When I first stepped into the round pen with him, he raised his head, snorted hard, and began galloping around the fence, looking for an escape. My very presence was unbearable to him, and I was worried he'd try to jump out. He was athletic for his size and could change directions and be gone in a flash. The slightest noise or movement set him off.

This one could be a challenge, I thought. But as he slowed for a moment and broke into a flowing trot, extending his long legs and pointing his hooves like a ballet dancer, I also saw enormous potential. This graceful animal could make a valuable jumper or dressage horse—if I could just earn his trust.

The black horse belonged to a woman named Helga, who I'd met some years earlier. She couldn't even get close to him, let alone get on his back, so she called me for help. After thirty minutes of working him, I finally got him to stand still long enough for me to touch his neck. I could feel the rigid tension of his muscles and smell his sweat. He towered over me, ready to flee, eyes wide with fright.

"He acts like he's been beaten," I said to Helga. "Do you know anything about his history?"

She shook her head. "The guy who sold him to me said he'd been ridden, but no one was willing to show me. I did see a club in the corral where he was kept."

I nodded, keeping an eye on the trembling horse. "That would make sense of his fear. The question is, can he get over it?" Once abused, some horses never forget. They're unable to forgive humans for the wrongs that were done to them.

When Helga brought the black horse to me, it was not long after I'd started doing public demonstrations at the Diamond Cross. I knew this horse would make a fascinating subject. I didn't know if I could get through to him, but I agreed to take him on. The audience gasped at his size and beauty when the trailer door opened and he scrambled out, snorting loudly. He had no rope or halter—all they'd been able to do was drive him loose into the stock trailer. Within minutes his glossy coat was streaked with sweat and dust kicked up by his galloping hooves. If he stopped for even a moment, his whole body quivered with fear, ready to bolt at the slightest movement.

"What's his name?" a man in the crowd asked. I realized that Helga had never told me. I just thought of him as "Helga's big black."

"What do you think we should call him?" I asked the audience.

"Shivers!" someone hollered.

Everyone laughed, sending the horse skittering across the pen. But to me, naming this horse was no laughing matter.

"That kind of name defines who he is now," I told the crowd, "but not what we want him to become." I've known too many horses that were named that way. When I was a young cowboy on a ranch in Nevada, I was told to ride a horse named Popcorn. When I asked why he was called that, the ranch boss just laughed. "You'll find out soon enough!" Wouldn't you know it—that horse bucked like there was no tomorrow. Each time you jumped him over an irrigation ditch he would pop like popcorn! I learned a lot from that horse, but I sometimes wondered, What came first—the name or the action?

When it came to naming the big black horse, I knew for sure I wasn't going to give him a name that memorialized his fears. "Let's give him a name we want him to live up to," I said to the crowd. I suggested the name Braveheart, after one of my favorite movies about the heroic Scottish knight William Wallace. It wasn't just a name; it represented the potential I saw in the horse and the way I intended to relate to him. It was exactly the opposite of his reputation and his actions. I knew he would need to find courage and heart if he was going to overcome his fears, forgive the wrongs of the past, and learn to trust human beings. And I believed that he could. If I'm going to work with a horse, I have to believe in him. If I don't believe in him, I shouldn't work with him.

The Power of a Name

Names matter, because names carry expectations. Many of the world's ancient wisdom traditions believed that knowing someone's name or giving someone a name bestows mysterious power over that person. And there is truth here, though it's not magic. The words we choose to use when describing a person, or a horse, are powerful indeed because they reveal what we believe. Our beliefs determine our actions, and our actions determine our destiny.

When I take a horse that other people have given up on and unlock its potential, it's not because I have special powers that other people lack. It's because I believe in that horse. And I work hard to express that belief in the words I use, and even in the way I think about the horse. Your words and thoughts will translate into your body language. Horses, being so sensitive, will pick up on your beliefs. It's a reminder that horses, and people, tend to become what we expect them to become.

Growing up, my dad rarely offered words of praise or encouragement. My older brother, Clay, was the prime target of his criticism. Dad picked on him terribly. "You're such a pig," he'd say. "I don't know what's wrong with you. You'll never amount to anything. You're a lazy slob." Sure enough, Clay lived up to Dad's expectations. His bedroom looked like a pigpen. Stuff was strewn everywhere, and it reeked. What came first? The words or the actions? I'm not saying that Dad shouldn't have responded to the mess. But what strikes me when I think back is that I don't once remember him telling Clay to pick up after himself, or not to eat without washing his greasy hands. He let him do it, and then told him how awful he was. It's not surprising that the labels stuck and then became more real.

It reminds me of when I'd watch someone working with a horse back in the old days, all the while calling him stupid, stubborn, or worse. They'd use real derogatory words. And yet, as the person training the horse, they really should have been pointing the finger back at themselves. Horses know how we feel about them, and their behavior will reflect it.

Sometimes the labels we struggle most with are the ones we give ourselves. When I met Jane's sons, Peter and Luke, they had been through a lot—multiple divorces, their home burning down when they were young, and tough financial times. Those circumstances weighed heavily on each of them, but particularly Peter, who had an obvious chip on his shoulder, growing up in wealthy Jackson Hole, Wyoming.

It wasn't unusual to get a call from the principal's office with another report of Peter getting into some kind of trouble. Generally, it was innocent enough, but it was the kind of behavior that reflected a deeper discontentment. Jane and I worried that he was embracing this reputation as a troublemaker, and that left unaddressed it could lead him down a bad path.

As Peter would tell me later, he felt underestimated in those formative years. He thought people only saw him as a pudgy kid with Coke-bottle glasses and spinal scoliosis. In truth, most people—even the teachers he antagonized—instinctively liked Peter and recognized his potential. But he saw himself as a poor kid with something to prove, which manifested in his acting out in school.

When he moved into high school, Peter was ready to change the labels he had given himself. He made what he describes as "a conscious effort to flip the switch on my identity." Instead of letting insecurity and anger define him, he intentionally chan-neled his energy into being "somebody other people would like to be around." He quickly climbed to the top of his class, was elected to student council and the National Honor Society, and was voted homecoming and prom king.

What I remember about those earlier years was instinctively knowing that "troublemaker" wasn't really who Peter was. He just didn't know how to draw good boundaries for himself, or respect those we drew for him. I had to be patient and let him find his way. And he did. Peter went on to study at the Univer-sity of Pennsylvania, build a great career in politics, and become a wonderful husband and father. I was touched one day when he told Jane and me that he was grateful we didn't come down too hard on him during those years.

"You didn't define me by the way I was acting," he said. "You called out the best in me."

When it comes to kids, and horses, words have power. Actions follow attitudes. That doesn't mean parents are always to blame when their kids go off the rails. People make choices for all kinds of reasons, and we can't be too hard on ourselves if those we love go astray. But we can always strive to see the good in people, to call out their highest potential. It's important to see not only who they are now, but who they could be. Even if they're acting out and need to be disciplined, you can do so in a way that honors their potential to change and brings out the good, rather than reinforcing the bad.

The old saying "Sticks and stones can break my bones but words can never hurt me" could not be further from the truth. I still remember the hurtful impact of words spoken by my father to my mother or brother. I often thought to myself in those days that I'd rather get beat with a club than hear words like that from someone I loved. Words go straight into your soul.

We're far more affected by other people's judgments and expectations than we may realize—especially people we respect or look up to. That might be a mentor or teacher, or someone who's successful in our trade or sport, or a leader we admire. If you've ever had a parent, a boss, a teacher, a mentor, a coach, or even a friend who deeply believed in your potential, you'll know how transformative that can be. And if you've ever had someone like that speak harshly or dismissively about you, either to your face or behind your back, you know how devastating that can be as well. Anyone in a position of influence or authority needs to pay particular attention to the way they talk to those who look up to them.

We create our worlds with our words. I sometimes hear other ranchers complain, "Why is it so hard to find good help these days? People don't want to work anymore. I could do the job quicker and better myself." Sure enough, these people never seem to be able to find good help. Jane and I, on the other hand, have no trouble finding good help.

The leaders I admire are full of respect and gratitude for the people they work with. And you know what? Those people live up to the expectations. It might not happen right away, but in time, it will.

Trust in Progress

Change rarely happens overnight—with horses or humans. Sometimes we might feel as if our faith in someone's potential is misplaced. I certainly did with Braveheart. At first, I wondered if the big black horse would ever live up to his name. He bolted at the slightest noise or movement. If I picked up any object, like a manure fork or shovel, he'd let out a deep groan and brace himself for a blow. I couldn't even spit or he would bolt. With a horse this powerful, that could be dangerous. The slightest mistake could end in disaster.

After several sessions of working with him on the ground, I

reached a point where I could touch and handle him without him bolting. I even managed to get on his back, and to my great relief, he didn't buck. He was still nervous, but making progress, so I took him into a larger pen where he'd have more space to move. I thought this would help him build confidence. What followed was one of the wildest and scariest rides I'd ever had on a horse. Braveheart took off as if I were a mountain lion that had landed on his back. I was merely a passenger as he galloped flat out around the pen. Any slight movement or shift in my body position only frightened him more. What if he stumbled and fell, and I was crushed beneath him or dragged by the stirrup? All I could do was give him the freedom to run and hope that he would soon realize it wasn't necessary to run quite as fast. Eventually, exhausted, he slowed to a trot, then a walk, and I was able to slide out of the saddle. My knees buckled as I hit the solid ground. The next day, we repeated the terrifying scene. And the next. What had normally worked with other troubled horses didn't seem to be working with him. He couldn't let go of his fear, and I was trying to manage my own and that of my wife, Jane, who thought I was crazy to take such a risk.

I stood by the corral fence one evening, watching the big black horse pacing nervously, and asked myself, "Is this worth it? Why am I doing this? What am I trying to prove, and to whom?" I hate to give up on a horse. I know that I'm the end of the line for many. But I can't help all of them. Was I expecting too much of Braveheart? Somehow, I couldn't bring myself to walk away, even though I knew it was a dangerous choice. I just couldn't give up on the potential I saw in him.

Finally, I called my old friend Tink for advice. After I told him about the horse, I asked, "What would you do?"

"Well," Tink replied in his slow and thoughtful manner, "not all horses are worth the trouble. But if you think this one is, why not try riding him two or three times a day, and just settle for the slightest improvement each time. If you allow him to quit on a good note, eventually he will start like he finished the time before. Just hang in there and keep doing the right thing." Taking his advice, I continued to work with Braveheart. At first his progression was almost imperceptible. He still continued to bolt and occasionally would stumble as if he were going to fall, causing my heart to skip a beat or three. But I noticed that each day the distance became a little shorter and at the end of the session he was starting to relax rather than simply slowing from exhaustion.

At one demonstration, Braveheart made a particularly dramatic change. Lowering his head, he followed me around like a big puppy dog. Then, with trust, he stood still while I got on his back and he walked calmly around the pen as I shook my slicker above him. Just a few weeks earlier, this would have been impossible. The crowd was elated with Braveheart's progress. Many of these people had returned again and again just to see him, touched by the story of this beautiful horse who was struggling to overcome his fears.

Among the audience that day was Braveheart's owner, Helga. She'd been coming regularly to watch him work, and she seemed to enjoy helping out at the ranch. As she and Jane worked side by side, Helga began to open up about some of her past trials, broken relationships, and disappointments. It was clear she had been through some difficult experiences, and as a result, she didn't trust easily. After witnessing her horse's breakthrough, she approached me with tears in her eyes, but when I asked her what touched her, she physically recoiled and wouldn't say a word.

By the end of that summer, Braveheart had not only lived up to but exceeded my wildest expectations. He'd truly earned his name. His fear had fallen away, and he'd become a willing partner for ranch work and long trail rides. I started training him over jumps and he showed great natural talent—so much so that a local jumping trainer offered to take him on. We were thrilled.

When we called Helga to tell her the good news, her response stunned us. "I don't trust that horse," she said. "I don't want to put any more money into him. Maybe I should just put him down."

This made no sense at all. She'd seen how Braveheart had progressed. Why couldn't she let go of whatever she had known him to be in the past? Did she really not believe he had changed? I tried desperately to come up with a solution, even offering to become part owner and cover his training expenses. But she braced up like a sullen horse, refusing to reason. She just kept repeating, "Grant, I don't want anyone to get hurt on him."

It was all I could do not to exclaim, "It's a bit late for that, lady!" I'd been risking my life on this horse for weeks, and she hadn't seemed too worried about it then. Now he'd gotten to a point where he was past being much of a danger to anyone. I'd had others ride him; I'd even had a twelve-year-old boy handling and grooming him. He'd come so far. It was obvious he had let down his guard and begun to trust. Why was she suddenly worried about him now? She couldn't seem to see what was right in front of her eyes. Finally, I offered to simply buy the horse from her, but she refused, agreeing only that I could work with him for two more weeks.

Braveheart continued to make progress, and we kept hoping we could convince Helga to sell. Then a letter arrived. In it, she accused us of trying to profit from her and the horse. This was a crazy accusation. Money was the last thing that was driving me. In fact, I had risked my means of making a living by taking him on. But before I could retort, Helga said that it had happened to her before: a man had bought a horse from her, told her it was worthless, and then turned around and sold it for a lot of money. She wasn't about to let that happen again. At that moment we understood that nothing we had done or could do would influence the situation. This was not about Braveheart.

Still, I kept trying. I called her, but she refused to speak to me. She picked up the horse and said she was taking him to another trainer. I was sad to see him go, but I was relieved he could continue to make progress. Then, a few months later, we received another letter. Helga wrote that Braveheart had not been mentally sound. She hadn't been able to bear the thought of him hurting someone, and so she'd had her veterinarian put him down.

Jane and I were devastated. After all the horse had been through, after all he and I had overcome, she couldn't give him a chance. Something in Helga's past experiences had prevented her from believing Braveheart had indeed changed. Not only was she unable to see his potential; she didn't recognize when he stepped into it, right in front of her eyes.

Forgiveness Is a Choice— but Not Always an Easy One

We see what we want to see—and sometimes, when we've been hurt, we just see the whole world as hurtful. So many of us don't even realize that we are perceiving life through a veil of mistrust, fear, and cynicism. We're holding on to past wrongs so deeply that they continue to shape the present. While Braveheart had conquered his fear and forgiven humans for the abuse he had suffered, Helga couldn't learn the lesson he had come to her to teach: forgiveness and healing.

It is often said that holding on to resentment and anger is like drinking poison and hoping someone else will die, and that forgiveness is a gift we give to ourselves. Both of these sayings took on deeper meaning for me in the wake of Braveheart's death. I had struggled most of my life to learn the necessity and power of forgiveness. My inspiration has always been my mother, Jeanne, who continued to forgive my dad for being so verbally abusive to her in the early years of their marriage. I believe the fact that she forgave him was what gave him the freedom to change. She didn't hang on to the past or insist on defining him by who he had been. And he became a wonderful loving husband to her, through many of her own hard times later in their marriage. Sometimes, during her final illness, Dad would say he couldn't live without her. And he passed away just seven weeks after she did.

Of course, it doesn't always work that way. Just because you forgive someone doesn't mean they will change, and you can't forgive with the expectation of change attached. But I do think that refusing to forgive makes it harder for a person to change. And it makes it harder for you to move forward as well. I didn't hold out much hope that Helga would change, but I did know that I needed to let go so that I could be free of the weight of those negative emotions. It was tough, though. Especially when Braveheart's fans showed up the next summer to see him and I had to tell them the sad ending to his story. I kept seeing that beautiful horse in my mind, and his potential for greatness. I knew how hard he'd worked to change because I'd been with him every step of the way. How could she have thrown all of that away? Why did Braveheart have to pay for the hurts that were done to Helga? These thoughts and questions ate away at me. I tried to move on and focus on the horses I still could help, but I couldn't get Braveheart out of my head, nor my anger at Helga out of my heart.

What I've learned is that forgiveness is a choice. It's not a feeling. "I could never forgive that person," we think. "I just can't." But to release yourself you need to make that step, even if it's only through saying the words. You may need to say it to the person themselves, or you may not. Maybe you just need to say it to someone you trust, or to God, or to yourself. You may have trouble getting the words out at first. Do it anyway. Words are the beginning of feelings. Making the choice to say "I release this person from my anger; I forgive" is one of the most freeing things you can do. It might feel fake at first. It might seem like you're lying to yourself. But if you just keep saying it, eventually your feelings will follow.

Forgiveness is one of the toughest and most important lessons we can learn in life. As with many things, it's easier with horses than humans. If a horse kicks me or bites me, I don't take it personal and label him a bad horse. I don't harbor resentment against him. I just know that he has something in his past that causes him to act that way and it's up to me to try to help him. I reminded myself that the same was true of Helga. She was just living what she'd learned, embittered by her past. As Braveheart taught me, there's extraordinary power in believing in a horse and releasing them from their past. And that's true with people, too, even if it's harder to do. Though Jane and I were hurt and disappointed, we knew we had to let it go.

Forgiveness doesn't mean you accept or excuse something that was wrong. But it means you judge the problem, not the person. It means you choose not to continue the cycle of fear, anger, and mistrust. If we don't forgive, we keep the destructive emotions alive. As the saying goes, hurt people hurt people. And hurt people hurt horses, too.

When I made the choice to forgive Helga, I thought about Braveheart and tried to summon up a little of his courage. To this day I often think about that magnificent and brave black horse and the lessons he taught us: how to face our fears, forgive, free ourselves from the past, and move on toward our destiny.

CHAPTER FOUR

Clear Boundaries Make Happy Horses

Respect is one of the greatest expressions of love.

—Don Miguel Ruiz

THE SMALL COMMUNITY of Moran, Wyoming, is one of the most beautiful places on earth. Our ranch sits in a lush green valley that stretches to the foot of the majestic Tetons, which rise dramatically in a series of jagged peaks on the western horizon. It's a view that never gets old. I love watching the moods of the mountains shift and change with the weather. At certain times of year, however, Moran is also one of the coldest places on earth. In fact, it's the site of the state's lowest temperature on record: minus sixty-six degrees on February 9, 1933. Old-timers love to tell stories of historic winters when elk froze to death standing up and cars were kept running day and night to prevent the engines from freezing.

Even a "normal" winter is tough for humans and horses alike. So as each year draws to an end, and the heavy snow and bitter cold settle over the mountains, Jane and I load up our dog, Gracie, and our horses and drive southeast to our property in Pavillion, Wyoming, near the Wind River Indian Reservation. The Native American tribes call it the Warm Valley—and while that might be a bit of an exaggeration, it sure is an easier place to spend the coldest months. Thousands of horses and cattle winter there. The view from our windows isn't quite as famous as the one up in Moran, but to me it's every bit as spectacular. And it has one great advantage.

At first light, when I get up, I can see both herds of horses in the pastures from my window and observe their behavior before Gracie brings them in every morning. I purposely built the house with the main floor upstairs so we could keep an eye on those horses. I could watch them for hours—and often do. If you saw me sitting there, you might think I was daydreaming or wasting time, but in fact, I consider it my education.

Most horses in a herd, whether there are five or fifty of them, will quickly figure out how to live together harmoniously and cooperatively. Horses are herd animals by nature. Out in the wild they will band together for safety, convenience, and companionship. So it's in their interest to get along—after all, arguing and fighting with each other takes a lot more energy and would distract from the essential business of finding food, protecting the herd from external threats (be they in the form of predators or rival stallions), and raising their young. They may need to work some things out at first, but pretty soon a band of horses will settle into a social pattern that works.

I often wish the same could be said of humans. Whether in

families, businesses, or communities, we don't seem to be nearly as good at figuring out our differences and learning how to live together. I don't just mean we've got to all be friends. In fact, one of the most important lessons we can learn from horses is that setting clear boundaries and establishing respect are essential to a happy herd—and, I would argue, a happy family, a happy team, or a happy society.

To the eye of a greenhorn, the view from our window might just look like a bunch of horses of different sizes and colors standing around. If you looked a little closer, you might notice them swishing flies off of one another; scratching an itchy spot for a friend; dozing in the shade or sunshine. Most of the time, there's not much excitement in the corral, unless it's breakfast time or a couple of the youngsters decide to frolic—rearing up and biting each other. But when you know the horses' language, the seemingly dull scene becomes fascinating. There's constant interaction going on, subtle communication and dynamics at play. There are older, more dominant horses that have been around awhile. They may mentor or discipline younger horses or those newer to the herd. There's always a leader who has earned the respect of the rest and become the alpha horse. From there on down there is a chain of command or pecking order. You can see this when they go out to the pasture at night— they'll each take their place in line. Every horse finds their place and feels secure there, from the top to the very bottom. The "bottom" of the herd doesn't necessarily mean the weakest—it just means that the personality of that horse fits there and is comfortable. There are particular friendships and rivalries. And there's a clearly established social hierarchy that's being reinforced through body language all the time.

Horses *like* this order. It's natural to them. They want a strong, clear leader, but they want one who is fair, not abusive. I think that's true of humans, too. We have an innate sense of fairness. If you watch how horses interact, you'll see that they naturally respect a good leader and will follow them. They relate to us humans the same way. If we're strong and clear, they'll follow. If we're vague and inconsistent, they'll question and challenge our authority.

On a particular day not long ago, I was sitting at my window with a cup of coffee, watching intently. I'd recently purchased a young horse and had just introduced him to the herd the day before. He seemed like a promising horse, with a beautiful silvery blue-gray coat (called "blue roan" in horse terms) that earned him the name Concho—a silver ornament found on a saddle or bridle. When I picked him up from his previous owner, I'd noted that he was in a pen with a couple of other two-year-olds like himself. I asked if he'd spent time with a herd, and the woman shook her head.

I wasn't surprised—a lot of folks keep young horses separate from the older ones—but I was disappointed. That meant more work for me, teaching this young horse some basic lessons in respect. It's understandable that people worry about a valuable horse getting kicked or bitten if turned out with a group of horses that are older and bigger than him. Unfortunately, they're setting him up for failure. What many people don't realize is that in depriving the young horse of the chance to learn to respect his elders in a herd and receive mentorship from older horses, they're making it more likely that he *will* get hurt down the line. He'll think he's tough because he can beat other youngsters in a fight, but he's overconfident because he's never been exposed to his elders. Sure enough, while this colt was accustomed to being handled and wasn't afraid of humans, he had a problem that was potentially more difficult to correct: a lack of understanding of boundaries.

When I got him back to the ranch, I turned Concho out with our herd of geldings (neutered male horses). I knew that they could do a better job of teaching him manners than I could. Sitting by the window, I watched as he pushed his way up to the feeding trough beside Freckles, my oldest horse and the undisputed leader of the herd. Like a cocky kid who has no idea how to respect his elders, this colt was asking for trouble.

Freckles is a kind and fair leader, but he won't stand for disrespect. He flicked a large white ear backward—a subtle but clear warning. Concho didn't seem to get the message. Why would he? He'd never had the chance to learn.

Then Freckles swished his tail—a more pointed communication. When he was still ignored, he swung his back end toward the youngster and lifted a foot.

Even Concho understood this: "Get out of my space or you will get kicked." Freckles established his boundaries, and Concho scooted away and looked for another trough.

Unfortunately, that wasn't the last time the young horse overstepped the boundaries, and sure enough, one of the other, less patient elders in the herd let him have it just above the knee, creating a deep puncture wound that soon became infected in spite of our care. This "lack of respect" resulted in a trip to the vet and a long course of antibiotics for Concho. I had to wait a few weeks while his wound healed before I could start working with him on learning some respect, for horses and humans. I wish he would have had the chance to learn those lessons more naturally, earlier in his life.

Respect Comes Before Friendship

Respecting boundaries is one of the earliest and most important lessons a horse must learn if he is to be accepted as a member of a herd, and if he is to become a good partner to humans. Our natural tendency is to think that if we are just nice enough to the horse then he'll be nice to us. But horses who are spoiled and overindulged tend to become pushy and difficult to handle. Like kids, they'll be rude to get attention if they haven't been taught boundaries. They get in your personal space, scratching their sweaty heads against your arm until they throw you off balance. They step on your foot or knock off your hat. They get in trouble because they don't know when to stop. When we fail to teach boundaries, we may think we're being nice, but we're actually doing a disservice.

I've seen over and over again: clear boundaries make happy horses.

Horses set boundaries with each other. So when you set boundaries, you're thinking, and acting, like a horse—making them much more likely to like you and trust you. Clear boundaries make horses feel secure and safe. Some people work really hard to gain a horse's love and trust, but once he gets confident and starts being pushy, they're afraid to set a boundary because they worry they'll lose his friendship and undo all the progress they've made. In fact, it's the failure to define a clear boundary that sets them back. If the horse loses respect for you because your behavior is inconsistent, a loss of trust will soon follow.

Here's a lesson I've learned the hard way: *If you compromise your boundaries for the sake of the relationship, sooner or later you will lose the relationship.*

It's been my observation that people need boundaries in the same way horses do. Kids who grow up with clear boundaries develop a healthier confidence in social settings. And after twenty-plus years of working with leaders, I've come to believe that when there are clear boundaries in the workplace, employees are more likely to thrive at their jobs. A common example of a boundary that gets blurred for too many of us is the line between work and home—and it's only gotten worse since technology has connected us 24/7 and the pandemic turned many people's homes into their offices. Soon the boss is calling during dinner and expecting the phone to be picked up. It's no wonder people start to feel disrespected and resentful.

In all kinds of partnerships, whether in business, marriage, sports, or any other field, setting boundaries and communicating them clearly makes all the difference. Yet it's been my experience that we humans are not always good at setting clear boundaries—and these days, our culture doesn't help. People are so suspicious of authority and defensive of their individual rights. In the process, boundaries are too easily toppled and respect gets trampled underfoot.

So many parents these days want to be their kids' best friend. But here's the thing: respect comes before friendship. You're their parent first, before you're their buddy. We've all seen what happens with kids who are spoiled, who get away with tantrums and bad behavior. Before you know it, they're teenagers who won't listen to their parents or teachers, or adults who can't hold a job or respect the laws of society.

I feel bad for kids who don't grow up with clear boundaries, because I know that deep down they'll likely be insecure. I know, because in many ways I was that child myself. My parents literally let me run wild. I wasn't taught to respect what we might think of as normal boundaries. When I decided I wanted to take my mules camping overnight in the wilderness at the age of ten, my dad tried to convince me it was a foolish plan, but he didn't try to stop me. And my mom, struggling with mental health issues, was often barely present. At the time, it seemed normal to me. I loved my freedom, but I had some crazy mishaps, too—including the time my dad's favorite mule fell over a precipice and nearly perished and I risked my own neck to get him out. Looking back now, as a parent and grandparent myself, I see that I was far too young to embark on those kinds of adventures alone, when no one had a clue where I was. I never let my own child do that. I believe that my lack of boundaries as a child contributed to many issues in my adult relationships until, with the help of horses, I got a better understanding of setting boundaries with other people and myself.

We often have families visit Diamond Cross, so I see these issues up close. One family brought three generations to the ranch to celebrate the grandparents' fiftieth wedding anniversary. They were self-made businesspeople who had built a successful family business that was now run by their children. As I like to do whenever a group visits the ranch, I met them in the parking lot with Freckles (who you'll remember from his tussle with Concho). He's the undisputed leader of my horses, but he's also a gentle giant—smart, kind, and patient. People love being greeted by a horse, and I think Freckles likes performing his ceremonial duties, too.

The van pulled up, the door opened, and a pack of grandchildren tumbled out. Before I could stop them, they ran under Freckles's feet, putting themselves in serious danger. One girl even grabbed him around a hind leg, as if hugging him. Any normal horse would have sent her flying. Thank goodness Freckles is as close to a saint as horses get, and he stood like a rock. His head went straight in the air and he looked at me, like, "What is going on around here?"

I pulled the girl away from his leg, firmly told the others to back off, and then waited a moment for the parents to step in and establish some boundaries. But they seemed to just think it was inconsequential. The grandparents also stayed out of it, though their expressions were more serious. So I took it upon myself, for their safety and my own protection, to get a little tough on those kids and explain to them why what they'd done was disrespectful and downright dangerous.

Throughout that evening, I marveled at the fact that people who clearly knew how to run a successful business and lead large numbers of people in the workplace seemed unable to set simple boundaries with their own children. These kids didn't listen when the adults were speaking. They climbed onto the pen where we had a wild and untrained horse waiting to be used in the demonstration. They even rubbed their faces in their grandparents' beautiful anniversary cake, completely destroying it. Jane and I were appalled. Yet the adults seemed oblivious to all of it. Some even seemed to think it was funny.

With children, the problem is not just that parents fail to set clear boundaries; it's that they don't let their children figure out how to navigate boundaries with others who are older and younger than them. If you leave a bunch of kids to play together, they'll work out their social patterns in a similar way to the herd of horses outside my window. The older kids won't put up with a lack of respect from the younger kids, and the younger kids will learn how to behave around those who are bigger than them. Of course, kids aren't always nice about how they work out their differences and can sometimes be cruel, so it can be wise to keep a distant eye on them in case of troubling behavior that might need an adult to step in. But I worry that in an attempt to protect our kids from being bullied or hurt, we've gone to the other extreme, rarely allowing kids to play without close supervision. I wonder if this does more harm than good.

As the leader of my herd, I try to allow my horses to work

things out for themselves, up to a point. But from my favorite seat at the window, I keep an eye out, and if there's a bully that's going to get someone hurt, I immediately deal with that situation. The bully gets tied up, or put in a separate pen for a time-out and a lesson in boundaries. If these approaches don't remedy the problem, sometimes I'll go so far as to get on the horse that's being bullied and then chase the bully around with a flag. I let the other horses see it happen as well so the bully gets humbled. If there's one thing I won't tolerate, it's a bully in my herd.

Be as Soft as You Can, but as Firm as Necessary

While a child or a dog that hasn't learned boundaries might be annoying and unpleasant, a horse with the same issue becomes dangerous. Even a small horse weighs five times as much as an average human, and I've had some bigger horses that weighed close to fifteen hundred pounds. You can't afford, even once, to give them the idea that they can push you around or climb on you. We once took a mare in for training that hadn't learned any boundaries, and before we knew what was happening she ran right through Jane as she opened the stall door one morning, shoving her against the wall and breaking her clavicle. Jane suffered terrible pain, two surgeries, and weeks in a sling, and to make it worse, we spent every penny I earned from training that horse on the medical bills. That's the problem with taking other people's horses for training—you don't always know what habits they've learned at home. These days, Jane tends to carry a flag or a whip when she's working with horses in a herd. Like Freckles swishing his tail, she can use it as a tool to get the horses' attention and reinforce her boundaries.

If a horse hasn't learned about boundaries from the elders in a herd, it's absolutely critical to teach him that boundaries are to be respected and there are always consequences for crossing them. Allowing a horse to push through every boundary that's ever set is not only dangerous for the humans involved, it's cruel to the horse. Again, we might think we're being nice to him by letting him do what he wants, but we're setting him up for a relationship of conflict with the humans in his life and for an escalating use of harsher discipline.

When I start to teach a horse boundaries, especially one that's been allowed to get away with much, I'll start with a simple warning, like a firmly spoken word or a clear decisive stance—just like Freckles starts with a flick of the ear—but I'm willing to do whatever it takes to establish respect. That's one of the core principles of my work: *Be as soft as you can, but as firm as necessary.*

Every horse is different, just like every person. Some horses are highly sensitive and want to please. Even a sideways look is enough discipline for them. A young, wild, or traumatized horse will need more space between boundaries so they don't feel trapped and panic. Other horses might need a firm hand to get the message across, especially if they've become dulled by repeated indulgence or inconsistent training. I'm never abusive, but neither am I afraid to apply discipline when needed. You always want to start soft, but if there's no response you add a little more pressure each time, and stick with it until you get a change and then immediately reward that change by releasing pressure and letting the horse think about it and hopefully feel good about the change he made.

In some situations, you can create a boundary simply with your voice. I remember watching world champion stock dog trainer Jack Knox at a clinic one time. I had never heard a voice with such an incredible range of communication. If the dog went the wrong way, Jack's voice would rise, increasing in speed and volume: "Ah . . . ah . . . ah . . . ah . . . AH!" The instant the dog came back, the voice would soften to a croon: "Goooood . . . good boy." He was so precise about the pressure and release, just with his voice. I couldn't make out many of the words, but the meaning was crystal clear, to me and the dog. The sharp distinction between right and wrong was never in doubt, and the dog responded remarkably. While border collies are named for the geographical border region between England and Scotland from which they originate, I think it's appropriate that their name also means boundary. They understand boundaries intuitively, and sheep or cattle quickly learn to respect the boundary the dog sets.

Setting clear boundaries is critical in all areas of life, but many of us are not trained in how to do so anywhere near as skillfully as those border collies, nor do we know how to enforce those boundaries when they're not respected. When people run right through our boundaries, we get angry and frustrated. But if we haven't been clear about them in the first place, what can we expect?

Sometimes people don't even realize they're trampling on boundaries. Being clear about your boundaries isn't a guarantee that people will respect them, but at least it sets the stage. Then you start out being as soft as you can, but you're willing to be as firm as necessary. And as Tom Dorrance, the great mentor of many natural horsemen, used to say, "It may take all you've got."

A Lesson in Boundaries

One of the great challenges when training a horse is to get rid of his fear and gain his trust without losing his respect. Too often, once a horse is no longer afraid, he'll start pushing you around. If you're afraid to discipline him at that point, he'll lose respect for you. A good horseman is always sensitive to the balance between discipline and kindness. I sometimes imagine that there are two lines drawn in the sand in front of me—one right up close to me and one farther away. The farther line is the line of fear. When you're first working with a horse, you're trying to encourage him to come across that line of fear—to get closer to you and be willing to trust. It can take a lot of hard work, time, and patience to get him to the right side of the line of fear. But once he's there, and he starts to trust you, sooner or later he'll cross the closer line—the line of disrespect. Now he's up in your face, not honoring your boundaries and potentially endangering you. What do you do then? Many people are afraid to discipline the horse because they've spent so much time earning his trust and fear they'll lose it. Indeed, when you do apply some pressure as a consequence of his disrespect, it's quite likely he'll get offended and flee right back across the line of fear. Now you have to earn his trust again and get him to come back. But it won't take as long, and when he does, he's less likely to cross into disrespect. Ideally, you want to keep the horse centered up between these two lines. That sweet spot—where he respects you but is not afraid of you—is what I believe Tom Dorrance meant when he talked about the horse being "right on."

The earlier you can teach boundaries, the better. It's much harder to go back and fix a lack of respect that's become habitual than it is to establish respect for the first time. That's why it's easier to work with a horse that's afraid and to earn its trust than it is to work with a horse that's been loved and spoiled and has no fear. A wild horse already has a healthy respect but needs to overcome his fear so that we can be friends and partners. A tame horse thinks I'm her buddy, but she might actually be more of a danger to me if she hasn't learned respect.

Take Velvet, for example. She's a beautiful, high-spirited three-year-old black mare that was bred by one of my neighbors. She's been shown love since the day she was born, but she's also been overindulged. Her owner, Karen, wants to be her best friend. When she came to me for training, the mare was a mix of clingy and nervous. She'd push right up against me when I entered her corral, wanting to be petted, but if something scared her she was liable to run right over me. My work with her would not be about earning her trust or overcoming her fears. She needed to learn that respect comes before friendship.

I brought Velvet into the round pen one day for a demonstration with a corporate group that was visiting. Spooked by the crowd, she naturally bolted to the side of the pen that was farthest from where the people were sitting and closest to the gate. Head high and tail rippling in the breeze, she paced back and forth, looking over the fence to the corral where the other horses were standing. They didn't pay much attention—they'd seen this show plenty of times before. The human audience, however, was captivated by the mare's antics and her good looks. I set up a simple but very effective training device to teach Velvet a lesson about boundaries. First, I placed a thick white yacht rope on the ground across one-third of the round pen, effectively dividing it into two sections, with the smaller section being the one closest to the audience.

"I'll need your help in teaching her to honor this boundary," I told them. "What we want her to do is stay on one side of the rope—the side that's closest to all of you. I want her to respect that boundary and not step over it and go to the other side of the pen, where she is right now."

That's not a small challenge, for several reasons. Number one, Velvet was loose in the pen without any restraints, and the rope was just lying on the ground, so it presented no actual barrier. Number two, the horse's instinct will always be to stay farther away from the crowd of people, not close to them. Number three, the horse knows that the gate on the other side of the pen is the way to freedom, or back to her security, which is the herd.

Using my flag, I drove the mare across the rope so that she was on the side closest to the audience. "This is where we want her to stay," I explained. "So the moment she crosses the rope to the other side, I want you to yell and holler and clap and make as much noise as you can. The moment she crosses back to this side—all four feet, not two or three—stop the noise completely." Noise is scary for a horse, so we can use noise in training as a form of pressure, and silence as a way to release the pressure when the horse does what we ask.

As soon as Velvet crossed the boundary and the commotion started, she bolted back across the rope. Silence. She stepped over it again. Noise. And back. Silence. It only took a few rounds of this for her to choose, of her own free will, to stay on the right side of the rope and respect the boundary. This comes back to another of my core principles that I mentioned earlier in this book (and will dive into deeper in chapter 5): *Make the right thing easy and the wrong thing difficult—and give them the freedom to choose.*

I was happy with Velvet's progress, and the crowd, as always, was amazed at how quickly she'd gotten the idea. By the time Velvet went home, she'd learned to treat me with more respect when I was handling her and riding her. She'd learned to honor various kinds of boundaries, not just a rope on the ground. Will she maintain it? That depends on how well her owner continues to reinforce boundaries, to insist on respect before friendship. It will be a challenge for her, I know. Karen's not too good with boundaries herself—she's liable to walk right up to some folks who are in the middle of a conversation and start telling them stories about her horses, unaware that she's interrupting. I hope that maybe some of what I said in the demo rubbed off on her, too. She truly loves her horses, and if she could just add respect into the mix, it would be so much better for all of them.

Boundaries + Consequences + Freedom to Choose

A boundary is not a physical constraint or a punishment. It's a line of choice with a consequence attached for crossing it. If my goal was simply to force the horse to honor the boundary, I'd put a six-foot fence across my pen, not a rope on the ground, or I'd tie her up so she couldn't get past the line. But that wouldn't earn me her respect nor would it be showing respect to her. The power of a boundary is that it is voluntarily honored—and doing so establishes a relationship of mutual respect.

For boundaries to work, they need to be clear, consistent, and have consequences attached. Then you give the horse, or the person, the freedom to make a choice. The first time I tried the boundary exercise in the round pen I just drew a line in the dirt with my boot. The problem was, the boundary wasn't clear. The big fat white yacht rope works much better because there's nothing vague about that boundary. But the rope on its own isn't enough without the noise. The horse is free to choose to step over it, but she quickly learns that the consequence of doing so is the noise, which she experiences as stressful. Because I'm consistent with this consequence, it doesn't take long for her to make the right choice. "You can choose the gate," I'm telling her, "but there's a consequence for doing so." When she makes that choice, I don't punish or abuse her or force her to go back, but I do apply pressure, in the form of noise. I show her that the choice she's made doesn't work so well for her, and I encourage her to search and find a better way. This only works if the consequences are consistent. If the crowd only made noise some of the times she crossed the rope, she wouldn't know what to do and would end up confused and insecure.

It's not enough to set a boundary once. When you present a boundary, along with the consequences of transgressing it, you have to be consistent in following through. People think it's okay to ease up "just this one time," but they don't realize how much damage that does. Horses don't understand vagueness. If you're vague with your boundaries, the horse will lose confidence. A boundary doesn't mean anything if it's always moving.

No doubt you've seen this with parents. I sure have. A client will roll up at the ranch with her kid, and while she's trying to talk to me about her horse, he keeps kicking the gravel at her leg. "Johnny, don't do that," she'll say. That's a boundary. Johnny will ignore her. "Johnny, if you do that again you'll have to go sit in the car." That's a boundary plus a consequence. But Johnny does it again and his mom doesn't follow through on her warning to put him in the car. She just keeps nagging at him, all the while trying to conduct a conversation with me. What's she telling Johnny? That she doesn't really mean what she says. Mommy isn't telling the truth.

That's how it works with horses, too. If the horse tries to snatch a mouthful of grass while you're out riding and you pull his head up, but then you let him do it the next time, you're telling him that it's okay to keep trying. So he'll be constantly pulling his head down and jerking you out of the saddle because he feels like a snack. If a tug on the reins isn't sufficient, then the tug is backed up by a slight spur in the ribs. If that doesn't get the job done, then apply a stronger spur, and continue to increase the pressure until that boundary is no longer crossed.

Back in my polo days, I remember one guy who struck me as a good horseman and a great father to his three girls. They were confident, secure, healthy, outgoing kids. If they got out of hand, he'd say their names in a certain tone of voice, and then he'd give them what they called "the look." That was all it took to get them to behave. Why did it work? Because "the look" was backed up. No doubt he had clearly established the consequences of ignoring it and had not been afraid to follow through on them.

Boundaries + consequences + freedom to choose: Jane and I applied this same formula when our kids were teenagers. We set a clear boundary for being home and in bed: 10:00 p.m. We also established clear consequences for crossing that boundary: no going out for the following two weekends. With these elements in place, we weren't nagging at them about the time or driving around looking for them when they were late. We respected their freedom to choose even as we were asking them to respect the boundary we'd set. At breakfast the next morning, we'd simply say: "I'm so sorry you made that choice, honey, but as a consequence of the choice you made you'll get to spend the next two weekends at home with us."

You Can Be Soft Without Giving Up Your Boundaries

A lot of people think of boundaries as hard, rigid positions. I prefer to think of them as soft but firm. You're not the one making it hard—the horse, or the kid, is making it hard on themselves by the choice they are making. Here's a simple example that shows this principle: When you're riding a horse, the reins are a boundary, as are your legs on her sides. If the horse pulls on the bit, she's pushing the boundary. You don't have to pull back or jerk at her, but you do need to hold the boundary firm. Your hands are soft but unmoving; you're not pulling on her. She's pulling on herself, and it doesn't feel good. So she'll search for another answer. She'll raise her head or lower it, root with her jaw, brace her feet, or even plow through your hand. You don't need to do anything but hold still and wait until she stops resisting. The second she does, you release the pressure as a reward for her respecting your boundary.

It's the same with the teenagers who break their curfew. You don't have to yell at them or get in a big fight every time they come home late. You can be kind and compassionate about the predicament they've gotten themselves in, without moving an inch. You're not the one making it hard. They are making it hard on themselves by choosing to cross the boundary even though they know the consequences. By staying soft but firm, you keep reminding them that there's a better choice.

Of course, testing boundaries is a natural part of growing up, for kids and for horses, so it won't always be an easy ride. It's how they find their place, how they establish independence, how they define themselves. When you set a boundary, you can expect it to be tested, and the fact that it is being tested doesn't have to be a problem. So long as you stay as soft as you can but as firm as necessary, the boundary can be pushed without collapsing.

Boundaries Can Bring Us Together

We often think of boundaries as dividing lines between ourselves and another, whether it be a person, a horse, or a dog. And sometimes we do indeed need to set a boundary in that way, to reinforce respect for our personal space. Used well, however, boundaries are not really about dividing but about uniting. They're about getting on the same page about what's expected, establishing trust by being clear and consistent. When someone respects you and gives you space, you feel closer to them than you do to someone who is in your face all the time, demanding your attention. That's why the herd of horses is able to live together harmoniously.

At times, a boundary isn't between us at all; it is used to say "Stay here with me" rather than "Stay away from me." Think of a mother taking her five-year-old out for a walk in the park. She lets him run a little way ahead of her, but not too far. She tells him he must stop before crossing a road, and that he must never get out of sight or out of range of her voice. Those boundaries keep them together, and they keep the child safe.

When you're working with a team, you might set boundaries about how individuals will interact and collaborate, in order to keep the team unified and aligned. For example, certain times can be set aside for focused work without interrupting each other, or guidelines can be established for how decisions are made and whose opinions need to be heard. Clear boundaries prevent conflict before it arises and allow the team to build trust and respect. In the end, as my wife, Jane, likes to say, a clear boundary is for the good of all. Freedom within boundaries is a safe place for work and play.

CHAPTER FIVE

Make the Right Thing Easy and the Wrong Thing Difficult

Where there is force, there can be no choice.

—JOHN JORTIN,
English theologian and historian

T HERE IS NO SUCH THING as a runaway," I once heard the great teacher Ray Hunt say. "I can ride as fast as they can run away." He uttered these words while galloping at high speed around a parking lot aboard a fiery Arab stallion. I'd just pulled up for my first clinic, and this was my introduction to the man I hoped to learn from. I watched as he just let that horse run, making no attempt to stop him, but continuing to direct the horse's feet around the parked cars and trailers as onlookers jumped out of the way. Eventually, the horse got tired of running and slowed down by itself. Ray praised the horse, slid out of the saddle, and handed the reins back to the owner.

I thought about his words recently as I led my horse Rooster out to the big round pen on our ranch. Rooster is a well-bred and handsome eight-year-old horse with a dark chestnut coat.

He's supersensitive and has a big motor. He also gets insulted real easy, so you've got to treat him just right. He'd already had a workout that day—a couple of teenage girls from the East Coast had been out at the ranch to ride, and I'd let them take Rooster for a spin. They're both very good riders, but they're trained in a traditional style that emphasizes controlling and restraining the horse. And when they run into a hot-blooded horse like Rooster and feel his anxiety, their instinct is to try even *harder* to contain his energy rather than to simply direct it. This combination led to Rooster fighting the bit in his mouth while they battled for control, and I was worried he might have picked up some bad habits. I don't want to have to fight or restrain my horses; I want them to *choose* to work with me.

"Sorry, son," I told him as I opened the gate and stroked the hair on his neck, still stiff with dried sweat. It was an unusually hot June afternoon, and I, too, had been working in the dusty ring for hours. Like the horse, I was ready for a break. But this was important. "You're not quite done for the day. I need you to come back to your foundation of trust, relax, and get in sync with me. Then we can finish the day on a good note."

I mounted up. And then, leaning forward, I removed the bridle and hung it on the fence.

On a highly strung horse like Rooster, that's a risk. Without a metal bit in his mouth or reins to slow or steer him, I'm giving up control. If the horse wants to run, buck, or pretty much anything else, all I can do is hang on. When I do this with my trusted friend Freckles in demonstrations, I know he'll take care of me and do exactly what I want. It's as if he reads my mind—in fact, I believe he does, or at least he picks up on body language that is so subtle it can't be seen. The more unpredictable Rooster is another matter. But I decided the risk was worth taking at that moment, to get the horse thinking and remind him of his freedom to choose.

I describe my approach to training horses as "restraint free." That doesn't mean I don't make use of ropes, halters, or bridles as tools when necessary. But especially at the beginning, I give the horse the freedom to move and the freedom to *choose*—which gives him the freedom to learn.

Many riders are afraid of a young horse getting out of control, so they try to restrain him all the more. This causes greater anxiety for the horse, and often he will resort to bucking, rearing, or other dangerous actions, not to mention bad habits like pulling on the bit, grinding his teeth, and throwing his head. When I ride a horse for the first time, I will ride him in a rope halter (which has no bit), allowing him a lot of freedom to move when he's afraid. I don't want him to feel trapped in any way. It's very important to always give the horse an escape route in which he has open space to run. This gives him confidence knowing that his life is not in danger.

My job as a teacher is to offer the horse choices and get him thinking. I want to get through to his mind, not just force his body to comply. I make suggestions and help him find the right answers, but I never force him to do what I want or restrain him from doing what he thinks he needs to do. When he makes the wrong choice, he runs into continued pressure or hard work as a consequence. When he makes the right choice, I let him think it's his idea and congratulate him for it by giving him a break or a rest, along with maybe a stroke on the neck or reassuring words. I believe that builds his self-esteem. Horses really appreciate this freedom and learn quite rapidly. I think we as humans are very much the same. We don't want someone telling us what we have to do or forcing us against our will. We accept instruction much better when allowed the freedom to make our own choices.

Freedom of choice is absolutely foundational when working with a young horse. Even with an older horse like Rooster, it's a lesson I come back to again and again.

Leaders often make the mistake of thinking that the shortest route to the outcome they want is to *not* give people many choices. Their logic is, "If I give people too much freedom, the result will be chaos. There will be too many mistakes and detours, and the work won't get done." So they build in layers of rules and oversight, trying to take as much risk and unpredictability out of the system as possible.

The problem with that approach is that it might work okay when the leader is breathing down people's necks. But as soon as the leader needs to be somewhere else, people will likely just slack off a bit. They don't feel like partners, responsible to follow through independently. And why would they? They haven't been treated like partners. And that's insulting to a lot of people. Don't you hate feeling like you have no choice, or like you don't even have the freedom to speak up and say what you think? It's disempowering, and it leads to resentment. When we do feel like we have a choice, we might not always like the options in front of us, but at least we have some influence on what comes next.

Treating someone like a partner means giving them a choice and trusting them to make good decisions. You can encourage them to make the right ones, you can make suggestions, and you can create consequences for whatever choice they make. But you can't force them. A lot of people bully horses, just like some leaders try to bully people. My approach is more of a negotiation.

Of course, giving horses or people the freedom to choose doesn't mean there's no structure or guidelines. It's not a free-for-all. I wouldn't try the bridleless exercise with Rooster out on a rocky, treacherous open range. I do it in a safe, well-contained pen with soft footing and smooth fencing. It's setting him (and me) up for success. Similarly, I believe a leader's job is to set people up for success by creating a learning environment where expectations and boundaries are clear but there is freedom within those parameters. It's always a balance you need to pay attention to. Am I being too controlling? Do I need to lighten up a bit? Have things gotten too free? Do I need to create more structure?

Honor the Freedom to Choose

One of the most powerful principles I learned from the wise Ray Hunt is "Make the right thing easy and the wrong thing difficult." It's what allows you to give the horse freedom and respect his right to choose while still getting the outcome you want. Horses are highly intelligent, and they know it's not in their best interest to keep doing something that is hard, stressful, painful, or exhausting. They're survivalists. Give a smart horse a better option—an easier option—and sooner or later he'll take it. Through respecting his individual right to choose rather than trying to force him to behave a certain way, a willing partnership is built—like the one I have with Rooster. He just needed a little refresher course that day.

Using my legs and waving my hat near his head, I got him loping around the ring, dust flying behind us. There are few things more exhilarating than riding a bridleless horse at high speed. It takes a lot of trust. As we reached the far side of the pen, Rooster turned and cut across the middle, back toward the gate. As he got closer, he slowed down. Like most horses, he wanted to stop at the gate and go back to his friends. When he got to the other side of the pen, he wanted to speed up and get back to the gate as fast as possible. I wanted to remind Rooster how to stop without fighting against his rider. And I wanted him to do it on the opposite side of the ring, precisely at the place where he wanted to speed up. I didn't have a metal bit in his mouth to enforce this idea, so I needed to put the philosophy to work. Make the right thing easy and the wrong thing difficult.

In this case, the "right thing" was being on the far side of the ring and calmly coming down to a halt of his own accord. The "wrong thing" was the gate. So every time we neared the gate, I urged Rooster to gallop faster, waving my hat, squeezing with my legs, leaning forward, and raising the tempo in my body. I was associating the gate with hard work. As he neared the other side of the ring, I sat deep and calm in the saddle, suggesting to him with my body language that I'd like him to slow down. Without reins, I couldn't pull him to a stop, but I could give him the idea. After a couple of rounds, he came to a complete halt exactly where I wanted him to do so. I ran my hand down his neck and let him stand there for a minute. When a horse makes the right choice, I like to give him a rest so he can think about what he just learned and let it soak in. This helps him remember the experience and learn from it. Rooster is a smart horse and this wasn't his first ride, so it didn't take long for him to figure it out. I repeated the exercise a couple of times, and then dismounted, loosening the cinch and rubbing his head and chest as a reward. He lowered his head, blew out a long sigh, and proceeded to follow me like a dog as I walked back toward the gate. We were both done for the day.

Beyond the Battle of Wills

There's no point getting stuck in a battle of wills. I believe this is true in all areas of life, not just in the round pen. But when it comes to horses, it's especially important because they're so much bigger than we are! Getting into a battle of wills with an animal that weighs ten times your body weight isn't likely to end well for you—and it's no good to the horse, either. We used to use the term "bronc fighting" for the old methods of breaking a horse, and there was a reason you didn't do it in public. It was exciting, but it wasn't very pretty. Another old cowboy term for a horse-breaker was "bronc peeler," because often the horse got peeled up and sometimes the peeler got peeled up as well. As in most battles of wills, one or both sides ended up hurting.

The key to being successful with this philosophy is to stick with it. You can't make the right thing easy and the wrong thing difficult just once and then go back to letting the wrong thing work for them. If a kid throws a tantrum and you give in and do what he wants, you're letting the wrong thing work for him. If a horse bucks you off and you immediately unsaddle him and let him go back with the herd, you're letting the wrong thing work for him. I like to remind the horse that bucking is hard work by driving him around and keeping him moving as long as he chooses to buck. As soon as he chooses to move forward freely without bucking, I let him rest and come to a stop. I once had a mare who wouldn't stop bucking every time she was saddled. So I loaded up a packsaddle with two fifty-pound bags of salt and then turned her loose in the corral. She was free to buck if she thought that was the best thing to do, but it sure wouldn't be easy!

In such moments, it's important to know that often things get worse before they get better. You'll think, "This isn't working." The tantrum gets worse. You feel like giving up. When this happens to me, I always hear my mentor Tink Elordi's voice in my head saying, "Hang in there!" He used to tell me this again and again when I was working with him and a horse was running through a boundary I'd set. Sometimes he'd have to holler it at me because I'd be flying across the pasture with no brakes. *"Hang in there!"* I'd hear him yell over the rush of wind and the pounding of hooves. And as soon as the horse responded with a shift—sometimes before I even realized that it had—he'd say, "There. Do you feel that?" Until you *do* feel that, you need to hang in there. Otherwise, you let the wrong thing work for the horse. Have faith in the process, and don't release the pressure as long as the horse is resisting.

As a leader, it takes wisdom to know when and how to apply pressure. Remember, the end goal is to set the horse up for success and help them come through safely. So be wise in picking your battles. You don't want to start something you can't finish. If you start trying to teach a horse something but stop in the middle when he's still resisting, you make him worse because you reward the wrong thing. If I have an issue to deal with, I'm first going to consider: Is it the right time for a conflict? And is it the right place? Am I somewhere safe where there's less likelihood of the horse or myself getting hurt? If I'm out on icy ground, or in a pasture with barbed-wire fencing, that might not be the best place to double down on a difficult issue.

It's easy to catch a wild horse—you can do that in five minutes if you're handy with a rope. But you've still got to get that rope off of him. That involves earning his trust, and it might take five hours. So don't start something you're not prepared to finish. This applies with people, too. Don't throw out a criticism or even a piece of constructive feedback when you don't have time to be there for how it lands. Don't ask a deep or challenging question if you're not ready to listen to the answer.

You Can't Force Loyalty

Harnessing the power of free choice turns conflicts into partnerships. When people or horses feel that you respect their autonomy and trust them to make the right choices even when you're not looking, they step up and become more proactive and responsible. Horses learn very quickly that the release they are looking for comes when they choose to do the right thing. In my work with horses, I've come to believe that true obedience, and even more important, loyalty, is only earned in freedom, within clear and consistent boundaries.

This is a lesson that has been powerful for many of the leaders who've watched me work. Good leaders know that they can't control everything from the top. Even if they wanted to, their organizations are just too big and complex, and things are changing too fast. Micromanagement slows everything down and makes employees feel resentful and disrespected. If I'm constantly looking over our ranch hand's shoulder as she's sweeping out the barn or saddling a horse, she'll feel like I don't trust her. But if she knows I believe in her abilities and trust her good judgment, she'll feel accountable even when my back is turned.

People need the freedom to make decisions on the ground and take more initiative. A good leader wants to encourage freedom, not constrain it. So principles like "Make the right thing easy and the wrong thing difficult" are great leadership tools. They help leaders empower people at every level of the organization to use their own best judgment, take risks, and be innovative.

Horses, like people, know when you don't really trust them or respect their power to choose. If you treat your horse like he's enslaved, he might do the job most of the time because he has to, but he'll resent it. I've seen so many horses like this. When I go out to the corral to catch my horses, I want them to come to me not because they have to but because they know that's the best deal for them. But if you haven't established that kind of bond with your horses, what often happens is that you go into the corral to catch them and they turn their heads away. They may let you catch them, because they know they don't have a choice, but they won't acknowledge you. You have control of their bodies, but not their hearts. There's no real loyalty in this kind of relationship and they'll leave you high and dry at the first opportunity. If your relationship relies on force rather than free choice, it's not really a partnership.

That becomes a real problem when you find yourself in a tough situation and you need to be able to count on your horse. A partner will stick with you through thick and thin. If you're out on the range and your horse steps in a hole and stumbles, throwing you out of the saddle, you're suddenly dependent on that horse choosing to stay with you. If he only does what you say because you have him on the end of your rope or a rein, that's probably the last you'll see of him. He'll see his chance at freedom and cut and run. You're stuck out there alone, at the mercy of the elements, because your horse was not with you mentally. His security is his herd and the barn, so that's where he'll be headed. At best, you might be facing a long walk home—that is, if you don't have a broken leg. But a horse that's really your partner won't leave you. He might be spooked or bolt initially, especially if he's scared, but in the ideal scenario, you're his security, so he'll stick with you.

When I was much younger, I had a job as a packer, which meant I accompanied people out into the mountains with a string of packhorses, carrying their gear, and then took the pack train home and left them to camp and hunt for a week or so before picking them up. This is called a "spot pack." One time, my clients were three veterinarians. As I was getting ready to leave them and their three riding horses behind, I gave them one critical piece of advice: "Don't drop your horses all at once." I knew that without someone holding their ropes, those canny old trail horses would feel no obligation to stick around.

I set off down the mountain path with my packhorses. As soon as I got home, I got a call from a rancher who knew I worked in that area. "There are three loose horses here at the trailhead," he told me. "Would they happen to be yours?" Those horses had traveled at least ten miles over steep and rocky terrain, dragging their reins. No sooner had I left those guys, they had dropped all three horses, and because those horses were only complying when forced to do so, they took advantage of that freedom immediately and left the guys high and dry. I had to lead those horses all the way back up to their camp the next day.

It might seem like a risk to give people or horses too much freedom. But there's a potential reward that is priceless: loyalty. Loyalty is much more than obedience or obligation. It's a free choice to stick with a leader or a partner, even through tough times or in the face of danger. In the West, there's a saying: "You ride for the brand." It means you're loyal to your ranch, come what may. You'll show up and do your part.

When I think of loyalty, my mind immediately goes to Freckles. In the more than twenty years we've been working together, he's learned that I respect his choices, his intelligence, and his instincts. I trust him with my life, and I believe he trusts me in the same way. He knows we're partners, which is why I can take his bridle off in front of an audience of hundreds of people without even a moment of anxiety. And he's not just obedient or well-behaved—he's deeply loyal. Over the years he's become one of my best friends.

CHAPTER SIX

Slow to Take
and
Quick to Give

Never discourage anyone . . .
who continually makes progress,
no matter how slow.

—PLATO

N OT THE EMOTIONAL TYPE."
That's probably how Dave Makowicz would have described himself when I met him. And the six-foot-four, two-hundred-thirty-pound navy veteran turned financial executive sure fits that description. Yet emotional was exactly how Dave found himself on the day he visited the ranch.

"This is one of the most important things I've ever seen in my life," he said, sniffing and wiping away tears as he stood beside the round pen looking at a sweat-streaked, dusty three-year-old colt that was standing in the middle, calm but still breathing heavily.

Makowicz was the chief operations officer for the investment firm CBRE Clarion Securities, which had sent its executives to Diamond Cross for a day to learn leadership skills. A couple of hours earlier, he and his colleagues had watched intently as I released the untrained colt into the round pen. The colt raised his head and cocked one ear toward me, eyes wide and gaze locked on mine. He wasn't scared exactly, but nor did he trust me. This was not a wild or traumatized horse so much as a spoiled and unruly one. He seemed to be trying to figure out what I wanted, but less out of a desire to please me and more out of a desire to manipulate me in order to get his way. His attitude reminded me of a surly teenager. He wasn't truly cooperating. He stayed as far away from me as he could, eyeing me from across the pen.

After working with the colt for an hour or so, I'd made progress. He was following me around and I decided he was ready for his first saddle. I threw a blanket over his back first, taking it on and off, getting him used to the feeling of something up there. Then I carefully swung the heavy saddle over him and let it gently settle on his back. The colt's ears swiveled back, but he didn't move. So far, so good. I pulled the cinch under his belly and fastened it to hold the saddle in place.

Looking across at the audience, I could see the skepticism on their faces. Some just looked bored. They didn't believe it could be this easy, and they'd been expecting more fireworks. The CEO later told me that at this moment, he'd been sure it was a setup and the colt had either been ridden before or was drugged. After all, who can break a horse to ride in just an hour?

If anyone was faking it, however, it wasn't me—it was the colt. I could tell that his cooperation was only skin-deep. I pulled the cinch a little tighter, then waved my flag to drive him away. All hell broke loose. As soon as he started to move off and felt the cinch around his belly, he exploded into a fury of bucking and snorting. His eyes were glassy with anger, like a child throwing a tantrum. He crashed against the fence panels, sending the Clarion folks cowering back in their chairs, skepticism replaced by fear. A couple of them even jumped up and moved to the back row. I could imagine them thinking, "Is he really going to try to ride that horse?"

I let the colt get his tantrum over with. I didn't need to punish him, nor was I about to get drawn into his drama and lose my temper. If I did so, he'd pick up on my emotions and it would only make things worse. My job was to stay steady and give him something to trust.

"Don't worry," I told the audience, "the corral is solid! And he'll get over it soon enough. I want him to learn that bucking is hard work. So as long as he keeps bucking, I'll keep driving him away by waving my flag at him—that's a form of pressure. Soon, he'll figure out that walking calmly around the pen or standing here with me would be much easier. And when he does that, I'll reward him by dropping the flag and taking away the pressure."

Sure enough, the colt soon tired of bucking and turned toward me, breath coming heavily through his flared nostrils. I immediately lowered my flag. When he got closer, I stroked his sweaty neck and told him, "Good for you. There you go. Isn't that better?" He'd made a step in the right direction and I made sure to let him know how positive that was. That way, I earned some more of his trust.

As the colt leaned in to my hand and lowered his head, signaling submission, I told the executives: "I don't need to punish his bad behavior. He already did that to himself. What matters is that I reward him for making a right choice. Honor the slightest try and the smallest change."

Another way I often put it is: be slow to take and quick to give. Too often, we're the opposite. We're quick to shut down or reprimand something we don't like, and we wait too long to reward a positive shift. We think it needs to be bigger. We expect a miracle. We miss the all-important little signs of change because they're not dramatic enough to catch our attention. That's how you lose trust. If a horse, or a person, is trying but feels that their effort is not being recognized, they often withdraw or give up. When I was a little kid, I had a football coach who quickly grew impatient because I didn't understand the play. He didn't realize I was trying my best and that I was terrified of failing in front of the other kids. I wasn't good at taking verbal instruction. I now understand that I'm more of a visual learner; back then, I just felt stupid. I can still feel it as if it were yesterday—the smell of trampled grass and sweaty kids, the rising sense of panic choking in my throat until I began to hyperventilate, which added to the trauma. That coach's frustration left a mark on my confidence that held me back for many years, and it became a pattern that I'd hyperventilate when I felt under pressure. I was a sensitive kid who wanted to learn but needed a different approach.

When we feel an acknowledgment of change, even if it's small, we feel safe to take another step, and another. An encouraging word, a compliment, a thank-you—these all communicate, "I see that you're trying, and I honor it." When people or horses feel seen and honored, they open up and try harder.

Horses are incredibly sensitive. They need to be prepared for each thing we ask of them, not startled with a sudden demand. You've probably seen those old Westerns where the cowboys come out of the saloon, run up to their horses, jump into the saddle, jerk back on the reins, kick them in the ribs, and take off at a gallop to chase the outlaws, leaving only a cloud of dust. That's the opposite of good horsemanship. It's offensive to the horse to treat him like that. Instead, we approach him slowly, mount up gently, and let him know that it's time to think about moving his feet. *Slow to take and quick to give.*

In a relationship of trust, we don't spring things on each other. Perhaps we need to have a difficult conversation, but we take a moment first to find out "Is this a good time? Maybe later would be better?" We give each other a heads-up if we need something done or need to make a change.

When someone breaks our trust, it's difficult to get over it. We tend not to forget those things, even if we want to, even if we know we should. Slow to take and quick to give protects the trust we've established, and it builds more over time.

Honor the Slightest Try
and the Smallest Change

The colt followed me as I walked over to the mounting block. Stepping up, I leaned over the saddle so he could feel me up there, all the while talking to him in a soothing, reassuring voice. I thought I'd earned enough of his trust that he'd allow me to climb on his back. Of course, with a wild or untested animal, you can never be sure. But there is a point where you just have to get on and expect the best. Face your fear, let go of control, and trust that things will work out.

First, I put one foot in the stirrup, pushed up, and stood balanced there on one side of the saddle. I didn't swing my leg over yet, but the colt was carrying my full weight. I leaned forward, making sure he could see me up there with both eyes so it wouldn't be a surprise when my leg appeared. He stood still, ears swiveled back toward me. I praised him again, getting down and petting him before repeating the exercise. This time, I carefully swung my leg over and eased myself onto his back. The Clarion group held their breath, waiting for the rodeo to begin.

I felt the colt tense beneath me. Was he going to buck? I didn't think so. If a horse is going to buck, you feel all the muscles in his back bunch up. His tail tucks in tight and his ears prick forward just before his head disappears between his knees and you are left flat on your back looking up at him, gasping to get your air back and wondering what happened. This colt was nervous, but he was starting to trust. The weight on his back felt unfamiliar, but my voice and the feel of my hand on his neck were reassuring. He took a tenuous step, and then another, and then he kind of scooted forward. The executives gasped.

I didn't grab at the reins or tense up. That would have signaled fear to the horse and broken the rapport we were building. I had to trust him in order for him to continue to trust me. This can be very difficult to do—especially if you've been bucked off or had a wreck before, which most horsemen have. You have to fight your own fear in order to stay relaxed, and you have to trust yourself. The more you've been hurt, the harder it is to get back on that bronc.

This is true in so many areas of life. You must *give* trust in order to *get* trust. If we don't trust a horse or a person, how do we expect them to trust us? A horse can sense when you don't trust him, when you're hanging on tight for fear he might buck or bolt. Old-style cowboys might have grabbed leather and gritted their teeth, but I tried to remain calm and loose, reaching up to rub the colt's neck. I didn't have a bit in the horse's mouth, just a rope halter to guide him. My job was to let him know it was safe.

"Easy, son. You're okay. You'll be all right. You can make it through this." To be honest, I was talking to myself as much as to the colt. But he got the message, and I did, too. I felt his shoulders and neck relax as he carried me around the pen. "There you go, good boy. Those are some good steps." I praised him again, and then dismounted and removed the saddle. He'd done more than enough for the day.

If you honor the little things, the big things will take care of themselves. But recognizing the slightest try is not always easy. If you have feel, you should be so tuned in to the horse that you sense when he's even thinking about doing the right thing. That's the moment to release the pressure and honor his try. Too often, our instinct at those moments is to do the opposite: to double down on the pressure and ask too much. A try might be almost imperceptible. If you're working with a wild colt for the first time, he might be too afraid to look at you. He's running around the pen with his head turned away. For him, turning to look at you is a try that needs to be honored. A glance might be enough of a change. You build trust with a horse by letting him know that you see him trying. And you let him know you see it by releasing the pressure. Often, that means it's enough for the day.

With horses, just as with people, never miss an opportunity to quit on a good note. It's important to accomplish as much as possible, but it's better to do too little than too much. Like doctors, good horsemen take to heart the message: first, do no harm. Often, trainers make the mistake of pushing horses too hard and end up finishing the day in a conflict or a drama. This creates resentment on both sides and results in resistance to further training from the horse.

Slow to take and quick to give. Honor the slightest try and the smallest change. These are phrases that have stuck with many of the executives who've attended my demonstrations—particularly CEOs, managers, and team leaders. They often tell me that, as they are watching me with the horse, they see flashes of their own leadership style.

"I realized I'm too impatient with my team. I sometimes miss the fact that they're trying as hard as they can."

"I think I emphasize the negative too much. I'm too quick to criticize, and I don't reward positive change fast enough. I don't honor the slightest try."

"I want people to trust me, but I see now that I don't trust them. I micromanage too much, so people get the message that I don't think they're capable of doing it themselves."

When Dave Makowicz watched my demonstration, however, he wasn't thinking about his employees or his role as a leader. He might easily have related the principles I shared to improving relationships with his team, suppliers, or clients, but instead, he couldn't stop thinking about his son, Nate. And about himself, as a father. Nate is autistic, and prone to throwing tantrums when he feels fear or frustration. Dave had a tendency to be overly controlling and get worked up in response. As he observed the transformation of the unruly colt, he wondered what it would be like to base his relationship with his son on these principles. To trust first. To praise the good and not be drawn into the drama when things went bad. To remain calm, confident, and consistent.

I waited until the crowd had dispersed before I approached him, sensing that the strength of his emotions surprised and embarrassed him. At first he had a hard time putting words to his thoughts. "I'm a controlling parent sometimes, with my son. Maybe I need to let go of the reins and just back off a bit. Let him be what he needs to be . . . and be there to love him when he's done." There was a brightness in his eyes, like he was already glimpsing a different relationship with Nate. "I see there is a better way," he said.

The horse still stood in the middle of the pen, looking like an employee who had made it through the first day on a difficult job. He seemed mostly relieved and maybe a bit surprised that he'd survived. In fact, he had done better than that; he had worked through his fear and inexperience and gained a confidence that things were going to be okay. I walked over to him, petted him, and removed the rope halter. As I turned and walked toward the gate, he watched me for a moment—and then followed.

If They Don't Trust Me, I Can't Help Them

Taking the time to build trust is foundational for everything else I do with a horse. Often, when they come to me, they need help. Perhaps they've been neglected or even abused. They may need doctoring. They'll have long, overgrown feet that are painful to walk on and need trimming. Imagine if your toenails grew unchecked for years, curling under. Now imagine your whole foot was a toenail. That's what horses' hooves are like. Unless a horse is running wild on rough ground, they need to be kept trimmed to prevent stress on tendons and ligaments. But to trim a horse's feet requires a lot of trust. She has to be willing to stand on three legs, giving up her ability to run or to kick. She's defenseless. A horse that doesn't trust won't do that willingly, and if you force her, you'll only traumatize her more. I need her to trust me so I can help her.

All the good intentions in the world won't get us very far if we don't have the patience to build trust. Sometimes well-meaning leaders will want to help the people who work for them, to lead in such a way that empowers others. But to be a true "servant leader" in this way requires some groundwork. You have to start from the premise that no one can be expected to trust you just because you would like them to. Trust must be earned—with horses and with humans.

One of the best, most trustworthy ranch hands I ever had was a man named Neal. This was back in my polo-playing days, when I was living in California. When I first met Neal, he was homeless, living in the desert. I'd often see him picking up aluminum cans along the road and collecting them in a burlap sack so he could make a few cents at the recycling plant. He looked like he'd had a hard life—shaggy-haired and hunched over, with a long, unkempt beard and tattered clothing. Beads of sweat stood out on his sunbaked forehead. His toes stuck out of old shoes. I felt sorry for him and one day pulled over and rolled down the truck window. "That looks like a heavy load you got there. Would you like a ride to the recycling plant?"

At first he stood motionless, staring at the ground, unwilling to make eye contact. "I'm going right by there," I said. "Be glad to give you a ride."

He stood still for another moment and then nodded.

"What's your name?" I asked.

The man said nothing. He set his bag of cans in the bed of my pickup and climbed in the back. *Can he speak?* I wondered. But I didn't press. He rode hugging his bag to his chest as if someone might try to steal it.

Periodically I gave the man rides, but I could hardly get a

word out of him. Again, I asked, "What is your name?" Without looking up, he replied, "Neal." I also learned that he was from Arkansas, but that was as much as he'd say.

One day I brought him a pair of new shoes and some socks, but he was nowhere to be seen in the area around his makeshift camp, which smelled like stale beer and garbage. Then a slight movement caught my eye and I realized he was hiding behind a tree. I didn't know why he was so mistrustful, but I wanted to give him space, so I pretended not to see him and just left the shoes by his tent.

A few days later I picked up Neal again. He was wearing the new shoes. The desert had already turned the white socks brown. I asked, "How would you like to come to our place and work for the day? I'll pay you twenty dollars to pull some weeds."

"All right," he mumbled, and climbed into the back of the pickup.

Neal worked all day in the scorching heat without stopping. He accomplished much more than I had expected. That evening I drove him to his camp and handed him a twenty-dollar bill. "You did a good job today, Neal. Would you like to work again tomorrow? I have horse pens that need cleaning."

He nodded.

"I'll come by about seven a.m." Neal didn't have a watch. "I'll honk the horn when I get here."

Neal began working for Locke and me regularly. Because our daughter, Tara, was only three years old, Locke insisted we be cautious. "Until we know he's trustworthy," she said.

Neal proved to be a very reliable stable hand, feeding horses and cleaning stalls and tack. He soon learned all the horses' names. Sometimes I would find him stroking them and talking. It wasn't long before he came to work for us full-time, and we gave him a safe place to camp on the ranch. The only rule we had to set was this: no drinking on the property.

"I hope you understand," I told him. "If you need to go get drunk, be sure you've sobered up before you come back, okay?"

Every couple of weeks Neal would collect his pay and disappear for a few days, but as time went by, he disappeared less often. When he returned, he would go directly out to spend several hours with the horses.

I always had the sense he was working through his issues and the best thing I could do was keep trusting him as he learned to trust me. Slow to take and quick to give. I also noted how the horses loved him, and they would gather round him any time he stepped into the corral. Horses are pretty good judges of character. Little kids are, too, and Tara always lit up when she saw Neal. Even with his small earnings, he would often buy her gifts, such as stuffed animals.

After many months had passed, Neal began to carry on short conversations, but he never talked about his past. We didn't pry. Before long, we bought a camper trailer to replace his tent.

Neal began attending church with us on Sundays. He was very shy around strangers; he would not talk or make eye contact. The people in our congregation always greeted him warmly and tried to make him feel welcome.

One Sunday in January, nearly a year and a half after Neal had come to work for us, someone from church gave him a bag of clothing. The following week Neal showed up at church wearing a brown dress coat and dress pants. He had cut his own hair and shaved his beard. Locke and I tried not to stare, but the change in his appearance stunned us. Neal no longer looked like a street person. Only Tara didn't notice a difference. She had known the real Neal all along.

Neal turned out to be a first-rate hand. More important, he became one of the family. Over time, we came to trust him so much that when we went to Kansas City for the summer to work, we left our ranch and several horses in his care, including Honey, a valuable thoroughbred mare with a broken splint bone. The vet couldn't help her, so he recommended putting her down. But Neal didn't want to give up on her and neither did we, so we left her confined in a small stall, hoping that complete rest and constant care would give her leg a chance to heal. When we got home, Neal was standing at the gate, smiling. "Honey's ready to go back to work," he said. She had completely healed in his care. Perhaps she helped him to heal as well.

About a month after we returned from Kansas City, Neal came to Locke and me, and said, "It's been twenty-five years since I've seen my family. It's time."

This was sad news. We were losing a friend and the best groom we'd ever had, but we were happy he was going home to be with his family. He had now been sober for almost two years. They would be greeting a new man.

With tears in their eyes, Tara and Locke hugged Neal and told him they loved him.

I drove him to the bus station, plenty early, and sat waiting with him for his bus. In the terminal, Neal turned to me and finally opened up about his past. All those years, I'd sensed he wanted to tell me about himself, but I'd never pressed. I think that's why he learned to trust. He told me how he had become an alcoholic, how he had felt so ashamed of himself that he had ridden the rails all the way to California, and how he had lived homeless all those years.

Finally, his bus pulled up and I embraced him. My voice cracked. "We love you, Neal. We sure will miss you."

Neal looked me right in the eye. "I love you, too," he said. "Take good care of my little girl." He walked away in his best suit of clothes, his hair neatly combed, his posture straight. Before getting on the bus to Arkansas, he turned and waved. Then he disappeared into the bus. We never heard from him again and I don't know how his story ended, but I never forgot him, or what he taught me. He was one of the first people with whom I applied the philosophy that I was learning with the horses. Helping him learn to trust and love again tilted me toward my life's work.

Of course, giving trust is not a guarantee that trust will be returned, and not everyone is worthy of trust. So I'm not suggesting that we should freely extend our trust to every person who crosses our path. I have had to learn this lesson the hard way. A few months after Neal left, inspired by his transformation, I hired another guy who seemed down on his luck—a homeless guy named Carl, whom I met outside the grocery store.

He ended up stealing a bunch of our saddles. "I guess you can't help everyone," I thought to myself. But sometimes, like Neal, people surprise you.

What I learned from Neal, as well as from so many horses I've worked with, is that trust is not just a feeling. It's also an action, and it's a process that happens over time. I like to use an acronym to remind me of the process of building trust—especially with a horse that's wild or traumatized and starting out from a fearful place. It goes like this:

T stands for Terrified. That's where we start. And you can't force an animal or a person who's full of fear to trust you. You've got to let them work through it. Be patient and give them the space and freedom to face their fear.

R stands for Resistant. Because the horse is terrified, she's resistant to your help. She doesn't want to cooperate even if it's for her own good. You haven't proven to her yet that you're on her side, so she sees you as a potential predator. Don't punish the resistance—you'll only reinforce it.

U stands for Understanding. The horse needs to understand that you're a good leader, that you're fair, and that you're not going to hurt her. She's smart, so she will figure this out if your messages are consistent. If you reward the good—honor the slightest change and the smallest try—she'll learn what you're looking for and start to work with you.

S stands for Submissive—and that's not a dirty word. It just means somebody has to be the leader and somebody else has to submit to that leadership. In the relationship with the horse, you have to lead the dance. Submission means the horse decides to dance with you. You can see the signs of submission in her body language. She'll drop her head and neck to the ground, and sometimes lick her lips. That's a breakthrough moment.

T stands for Trust—which is the result of the process you've just been through. A relationship of trust is a relationship that can last forever. It allows you to help the horse and teach her how to be a trustworthy partner to other humans, which is the key to her having a happy, secure life—a life that is the opposite of the kinds of experiences she may have had before she came to you.

Trust Takes Time

When a horse, or a person, has been traumatized or abused, it's perfectly understandable that they lose trust—not just in the person or situation that hurt them; they don't trust anyone, period. I've seen this particularly in veterans suffering from PTSD. Sometimes, they've lost their faith that life is worth living.

One time, I was asked to do a demonstration for a group of Iraq War vets. There were about eight of them, and they stood watching with curiosity as I released a wild horse into the pen. I began my demo, but something didn't feel right. These men standing around the fence were my heroes. They'd been willing to pay the ultimate price. They weren't afraid of a wild horse; they'd faced death. Who was I to stand in there talking to them on the other side of a fence?

The answer came to me in a flash: "I need to get these guys in here."

So I opened the gate and asked them all to step inside the pen. As each man came in, I shook his hand and introduced myself. The last man to step through was a big guy. He shook my hand but had trouble meeting my eye. Quietly, he said his name was Richard. I instructed the men to space themselves out around the pen. "Stand still," I told them, "and don't make any sudden moves."

The little mare, wild-eyed and panicked, tried to dodge between them. I was confident that she was so afraid, she wouldn't try to kick one of them as long as we gave her an escape route and didn't make her feel claustrophobic. I waved my flag and began to drive her. I was the source of pressure, the bad cop, so she began seeking something or someone for security. Slowly, she began to feel comfortable that none of the men standing motionless in the pen were going to hurt her. First, she'd just stop in front of them and take a good look. She began to trust enough that she'd reach out and smell one and then another.

"Don't try to touch her," I told them. "Let her touch you first. Reaching out too quickly will scare her." Soon, she started to reach out her neck, to sniff, and then to touch. The experience of this wild animal extending her trust toward them was so powerful for these wounded men. I could see them letting down their defenses, softening. During the course of an hour, I got the filly to connect with each one of them individually—except Richard.

She refused to go near him. Every time I tried to send her his way, she'd snort violently and spin around and go to another. He wasn't doing anything, just standing there, but she was terrified of him in a way she wasn't of the others. Finally, the big man got angry and stomped out of the pen, muttering under his breath.

I released the horse, but the situation troubled me. I didn't want to just leave Richard out there, any more than I like to give up on a tough horse. I asked one of the other vets to tell me about the big man. When I heard his story, I knew I had to try to get him back in the ring. Richard had previously attempted to kill himself but had failed. He'd shot himself in the head and somehow survived. So he was mad at the world, and angry that he couldn't even finish himself off properly. Now I understood his response. He already felt like a failure, and the horse's refusal to trust him was just another sign of rejection—proof that he was worthless.

I sought out Richard, over in the parking lot, and persuaded him to come back into the pen. I asked him to trust me—and although it was clearly hard for him, he agreed.

I stood in the pen with the big man and the wild filly. Life had been tough on them both, but I hoped they could help each other find a better path forward. I started driving her around, but she stayed as far away from Richard as possible.

"If she even so much as looks at you," I told him, "I want you to step away. Be quick to give. Release the pressure." After a few minutes, she was willing to turn her head in his direction.

"That's good," I encouraged him. "Step back again." Soon, with tentative steps, she was following him as he slowly backed across the pen.

"Now I want you to get down low. Squat down on your knees. Let her know that you trust her not to hurt you." He looked at me like I was crazy. Why would he get down in the dirt in front of a wild horse that didn't trust him? But he did as I instructed, crouching down, making his muscular body smaller and less intimidating. The filly approached, curiosity beginning to overcome her wariness. She reached out her nose and sniffed him, breathing into his face.

"Breathe back to her," I told him. "That's how horses introduce themselves. If she'll share your air, that means she's willing to trust you."

I saw a change in the big man's demeanor as he softly raised his hand to stroke the filly's neck. Gently, slowly, with no sudden movements, he connected with her. I had to rub a tear from my eye as I watched her standing there, her nose in his big black beard. Both of them seemed relieved. Both of them were learning to trust. It might take a long time for either of them to decide that the world is a safe place, but as they breathed each other's air, they'd at least tasted the possibility.

CHAPTER SEVEN

It's Not About Today, It's About the Rest of Her Life

Nothing valuable can be lost by taking time.

—ABRAHAM LINCOLN,
first inaugural address

I T WAS A COLD FALL DAY at the ranch, with a snow squall howling down the valley. The horses huddled together, backs to the wind and heads low. There are always a couple of weeks at the beginning and end of our season when the weather is a bit dicey, and this was one of those times. We had a group of top investment advisers visiting for the day, and winter had decided to make an early appearance. They hadn't just come for a demonstration; their program included some hands-on exercises like catching horses. So there we were, out in the pasture behind the barn, with a bunch of cold, miserable, underdressed finance guys who looked like they'd rather be just about anywhere else, and a bunch of equally cold, miserable horses.

One guy, however, seemed like he'd have been happy to stay out there all day. He was as bright and chipper as if it had been a summer afternoon. He introduced himself as Steve Story, and proceeded to bombard me with questions about the horses, about what I was doing, and about how my training methods worked. In his excitement to learn, he seemed oblivious to the wet, blowing snow and chilly wind.

When the exercise was complete, I was as ready as our guests to return to the warmth of the barn for the demonstration. But I knew it was going to be a bit of a challenge. The horse I was using that day was a tough one. I'd borrowed him from a friend, who had bought him cheap from a guy that raised horses for the rodeo. This two-year-old had been bred to buck, but he hadn't shown enough natural talent for the sport. Bucking horses are tested early by being put in a chute, saddled and flanked, sometimes with a light dummy on their backs, and then released into the ring. If they don't buck out well, they'll be sold off. That's what happened to this horse. He'd had a difficult start in life. Maybe if we went back to basics, I could help him find a better path.

A Strong Foundation Lasts a Lifetime

The first couple of years in a horse's life are when you build their foundation. Training a horse is like building a house. You put a brick in that foundation every day. Sometimes they're small bricks that fill in the gaps, other times they're big cornerstones.

If the house is to stand for many years to come, you can't afford to leave any holes in that foundation. That's why it's important to work a young horse consistently, on a daily basis. For the horse, those cornerstones are things like trust, discipline, respect, boundaries, and work ethic. Once you get the foundation solidly in place, the house will go up pretty fast, but if you leave holes, they'll appear later on and the whole thing might come tumbling down.

A great horseman once told me a horse will always go back to her foundation when she's under pressure. You'll see what she's made of. Sometimes you get a horse and you can tell someone left some holes there. Perhaps she's head-shy, or doesn't want her ears touched, or she's liable to kick when you tighten the cinch. All of these are foundational bricks that should have been worked out in her early training. It's much harder to fix them later. In fact, when I work with horses that are older and have been started poorly, I don't try to fix their specific problems. I just go back to the beginning and treat them like they've never been touched. I try to put them on a brand-new track, one that is built on freedom rather than restraint, on trust rather than fear.

It takes a lot of time and patience to build, or rebuild, a foundation. But I always remind myself: *It's not about today; it's about the rest of her life.* When I'm working with a horse in the round pen, I'm not doing it for the particular audience that's visiting that day. I'm doing it for the horse. I'm thinking way down the road, building a foundation for her future. I often tell the crowd: As much as I'd like to impress you in this demon-stration, it's more important that I impress the *horse*. The lessons she needs to learn will ensure that she'll be a good partner to the humans in her life, over the long run.

As Tink Elordi used to say, "It's not just about getting the job done." It's too easy to be focused on getting the job done that day. You get in a hurry; you get pushy. But if you scare that horse or push her too far, you'll make the job harder down the road. You have to prioritize the horse over the job. That sounds obvious, but it's so easy to let pride or impatience get in your way. For the sake of getting the job done today, you may dam-age a horse for the rest of her life.

Much of what we do when we're working in the round pen is about preparing horses for the real world. That's why we put in the hours of work—because if we do it well, it will serve to keep us safe in all kinds of situations. Earning her trust so she freely follows me around the pen isn't just a feel-good moment—it's about establishing a connection so that she won't leave me high and dry if I let go of her rope somewhere out in the back-country. Teaching her to tolerate a rope around her leg and to lift her foot on command isn't a trick—it's essential so that I can trim her feet and keep her sound and free from pain. Getting her to stand calmly with a flapping tarp on her back isn't about the tarp—it's about the slicker I'm going to need to pull on when I'm out moving cattle and a storm comes in. One of my favorite cowboy poems, which I often recite in my demonstra-tions, warns of the consequences of failing to put this particular foundation stone in place:

It's Not About Today, It's About the Rest of Her Life

When you're bustin' out a bronco
You better get him slicker broke
Or you'll have to do it sometime
*And it won't be any joke.**

The poem goes on to paint a vivid picture of what it's like to try and get a slicker on in the saddle of an unprepared horse when a storm is rolling in. You can imagine how it ends. It always gets a laugh from the audience, and the investment planners at the ranch that chilly fall day were no exception. Perhaps the hour they'd just spent out in the snow had made the necessity of a slicker particularly apparent to them. Thankfully, the demonstration took place in the barn, so we were no longer at the mercy of the elements.

I had a pretty good session with the young horse. Besides being herded into that chute and provoked to buck, he'd barely been handled. I spent some time earning his trust and getting him to accept a halter, then threw a heavy blanket over his back. I left it at that for the day—*always quit on a good note.* I knew it would take a lot more time and patience to build that horse a

---

* The tradition of cowboy poetry dates back to the mid-1800s, when working ranch people began writing, reciting, publishing, and performing poems about their way of life. Many cowboy poems are passed down through an oral tradition, and as a result, there are numerous variations on popular works. I learned this particular poem from cowboys I worked with, and I quote it here as I learned it. The original version of this poem, "Git Him Slicker Broke" by Bruce Kiskaddon, appeared in the book *Rhymes of the Ranges and Other Poems* (published by the author in 1947).

new foundation. There was no point in pushing him too far in one day. Hopefully, his owner would keep up the good work, or he'd find his way to a home that would. I stroked the horse's neck and told him he'd done well, then let him out of the round pen.

The financial advisers headed for the bar and the buffet— except one. Steve Story was waiting for me at the gate, his eyes lit up at what he'd just witnessed.

"Is that horse for sale?" he asked me.

Surprised, I told him that it probably was. "But I'm not sure you want to buy that horse." He struck me as someone with a lot more enthusiasm than experience when it came to horses, and the young horse was no fit for a beginner. "Why don't you tell me a little about what you're looking for?"

We sat down and Steve told me why the day had affected him so much.

"My sweetheart, Lori, has been through a rough time," he said. "She got out of a very bad marriage not long before I met her, and now she's had a falling-out with her father. She loves horses. I think that owning one and working with it might help her to heal." He explained that Lori had been born one of eleven siblings. Her father was a dairy farmer and always kept horses. As the only girl in the family who showed an interest in riding, Lori loved having a way to connect with her father, and one of her favorite things to do was to ride alongside him when he moved the cattle from mountainside to mountainside.

"Now that link has been broken," he said. After Lori's divorce, which her father didn't approve of for religious reasons, he'd sold the horse that had been Lori's without even telling her. She'd been devastated. "I just thought, maybe it would benefit Lori to reestablish that connection with a horse," Steve concluded.

I was touched by Steve's obvious love and concern for Lori. I was also firmly convinced that the last thing she needed was some failed rodeo bronc. That horse had his own healing and rebuilding to do. The image of another horse popped into my mind, taking me by surprise. I hadn't been planning on selling him anytime soon, but for some reason I had a strong sense he might be the horse for Lori. Jubal was a young chestnut gelding we'd bred on the ranch. His mother, Jewel, had been with us for years. Jubal had a sweet disposition and the best foundation a horse could ask for. We'd handled him since the day he was born, building trust, setting clear boundaries, helping him make good choices and gain confidence. He'd never had a bad experience or been treated with anything but kindness. If there was a horse that could help a troubled woman to heal, Jubal could well be the one.

"I might have another horse that would work for you and Lori," I told Steve. "If you're serious about it, why don't you give me a call in the next few days, and we can talk further."

I wasn't sure I'd ever hear from him again. Once he left the ranch and the excitement of the day wore off, perhaps he'd think better of the idea. But to my surprise, within a couple of weeks, Steve called. I told him about Jubal, sent him a picture, and we agreed on a price. Steve would bring Lori to meet the horse, and if that went well, I'd train Jubal for her and also teach her how to work with the young horse.

Steve told Lori nothing of his plan. He wanted to surprise her. Instead, he casually invited her to join him on a business trip to Wyoming.

"Do you think we'll see some horses up there?" she asked him.

"I think we might," he replied.

By this time, Jane and I had moved south to spend the winter months at our home in Pavillion. Steve and Lori drove up from Utah. My first impression of Steve's sweetheart, as he always calls her, was an intensely shy woman, her dark hair pulled back in a ponytail. She reminded me of a frightened horse that's had a difficult start in life—quite the opposite of her talkative, confident, energetic partner. She still had no idea why they had come, but she was drawn to the horses like a magnet.

"Can I go in?" she asked softly. I opened the gate to the corral where our herd of geldings were standing. She stepped inside, looking around with wide eyes at the twenty or so horses, who seemed uninterested in this stranger. Then one horse lifted his head, walked out of the herd, and came right up to Lori. He reached out his head to sniff her. I turned to Steve, amazed.

"That's the one," I told him. "That's Jubal."

"Hey, honey, what do you think of that one?" Steve asked Lori. She turned to look at us, her face lit up with pure delight.

"He's a good-looking horse," she replied, reaching out to scratch Jubal's neck.

"Well, he's yours, if you like him."

Lori and Jubal bonded from the start. Later, she shared with me what he meant to her. "For me, he represented a hope. Something to look forward to and something that was my own.

Something I didn't have to depend on a man for. When I was young, my dad was in charge of the horses. I never learned how to train them the way that you do. It was an empowering thing for someone to teach me how to teach Jubal, and to be able to make him do what I needed him to do without forcing it on him."

The emotional scars of her divorce were still very fresh. "My ex-husband just broke me down," she said. "After twenty-four years I was broken. I put up with a lot of things, and when I decided to leave, it got worse. Leaving him was one of the hardest things I've ever done." A powerful figure in their church, her ex-husband turned former friends against her and even hired a private investigator to follow her. "I basically left with nothing, just to get away from him," she recalled. "It felt like starting all over." To make it even harder, she'd never gone to college, established her own career, or had to support herself and her two children. In high school, she'd been a gifted track athlete and won a college scholarship, but a motorcycle accident in her senior year derailed those plans. She abandoned her hopes of going to college, knowing that her family couldn't afford to pay. Marriage and children soon followed.

When Lori met Steve, it was not long after her divorce. She was working in a physical therapy clinic in the same building where he worked. For eight months, Steve watched the quiet woman with the bouncy ponytail walk past his window each day and wondered what story was behind the sadness in her face. Privately, he thought of her as the "ponytail goddess." Finally, a power outage in the office gave him an excuse to go and talk to her, and the next day, he asked her out to dinner.

Steve told me some of this story during their early visits to the ranch. He watched intently from the fence as I worked with Lori and Jubal on some of the foundational lessons that build the connection between horse and rider. Jubal is a sweet-natured horse, but he was young and inexperienced, so we were still working on the cornerstones. *Respect comes before friendship. Make the right thing easy and the wrong thing difficult. Honor the slightest try and the smallest change. Be slow to take and quick to give.*

Despite Lori's shyness, she never seemed afraid when working with Jubal. "I feel at home on a horse," she told me. "Even on a horse that's untrained, I feel safe. I've never been nervous on a horse. There's something about connecting with an animal—it's a calming thing." I could see how happy it made her—and how happy it made Steve to see that the crazy impulse he'd had that day in the snow had worked out so beautifully. It was everything he'd hoped for. But, he says, "I had no idea that within a short period of time, something would happen that would change her life forever. And this horse would end up being even more important to us, in ways I'd never imagined."

Every Second Counts

Just a few weeks after Lori met Jubal, she and Steve traveled to Wausau, Wisconsin, to spend Thanksgiving with his family. On December 1, she wasn't feeling too well—in fact, she'd not been feeling like herself for a few weeks. Steve was worried, and told her that she should eat something, so he brought her some soup. He remembers her saying the soup was too hot, so he went back downstairs to get her an ice cube. When he came back up a few minutes later, he heard Lori take a deep gasp of air, and then her head collapsed forward and she slumped over. Steve rushed to her side, but her body was limp and heavy in his arms. He felt for a pulse—nothing. Her heart had stopped.

Frantically, Steve dialed 911 and the operator walked him through doing chest compressions. Still, Lori was unresponsive. "She was clinically dead," he says. "I'd literally heard her take her last breath." Within just minutes, he heard the sound of sirens, and two paramedics rushed in and took over CPR. Incredibly, they were able to restart Lori's heart and get her to the local hospital. "If they'd taken any longer, I don't think she'd be with us today," Steve says. "But they got there in just three minutes."

Lori remembers nothing of the incident, or the eleven days afterward that she spent in a medically induced coma. She'd suffered a cardiac arrest, and some damage to her brain as a result. Her memory starts to reemerge around day fourteen, but even then she's not sure how much is just because she's seen pictures and videos from those days. In the videos, she doesn't sound like herself. Her sister thought it was the drugs, but Lori says no, it was just because she was learning how to speak again.

That wasn't the only thing she had to relearn. Steve remembers watching her take tentative, wobbly steps across the hospital floor, as if she'd never walked before. "At first she stumbled, but then the physical therapist got her stabilized and she made a little loop around the nurses' station. And everyone cheered and encouraged her. I remembered you saying, *Honor the slightest change and the smallest try.* That's what you have to do when someone is starting from scratch. Imagine if those words were on every physical therapist's wall."

Almost three weeks after the heart attack, Lori was wheeled down to the hospital exit, and she saw the paramedics who had saved her waiting by the door. She and Steve left the hospital in the same ambulance that had brought her in, and they stopped at the fire department to celebrate with a cake and thank the heroes who brought her back to life. Without them, she'd never have seen another Christmas.

But Lori was only at the beginning of her long road to recovery. In the weeks and months that followed, Steve often found himself thinking back to their sessions with Jubal in the round pen. He remembered me talking about the importance of building a foundation, and how I sometimes had to go back and start over with a horse. That's what he saw his sweetheart doing.

"Lori had to start from scratch. She had to rebuild those skills. I thought it would be easier for her because the skills would be familiar, but I had to realize she was essentially starting over. If we've made any mistake with her, it's been assuming that she could go back to things too quickly. If you go too fast, then when something goes wrong, it creates a setback, and it's emotionally uncomfortable. When she'd fall, it was devastating, because she didn't have that foundation." Rebuilding that foundation will take a lot of patience and a long-term view. *It's not about today; it's about the rest of her life.*

He Makes Me Feel Understood

Jubal has played an important role in Lori's recovery, and continues to do so. Some months after she got out of the hospital, she and Steve came to the ranch to see her horse. I'd saddled Jubal and then turned him loose in a corral while I waited for them to arrive. Steve, as always, had plenty to say, and I was standing talking with him by the fence when I noticed that Lori had entered the corral where Jubal was waiting. After greeting the horse, she took a couple of steps in one direction, and the horse followed her. She stopped and looked at him, and then changed direction. He followed again. Soon, she was walking slowly in circles and figure eights with Jubal following closely behind her, head right alongside hers. It was hard to say who was training whom, but both were building their foundation.

"There's just a connection there," she told me later. "It's like he knows when I'm nervous or shaky. It's a connection that most people don't get with a horse—at least, I don't think I ever had that before. It makes me feel understood."

This summer, we had Jubal back in training. It was time to build on that strong foundation we'd put in place and make sure he was ready to partner with Lori in the next stage of her recovery. She's arranged to board him at a local barn near her home in Utah, and she is looking forward to using him to move cows with her father like she used to do when she was a little girl.

"My dad's getting older and not doing so well, health-wise," she explains. "I don't know how many years we'll have left, but we'll take advantage of them while we have them. I know he doesn't approve of all my choices, but I've just decided that I can't worry about what other people think. I try to let go of that concern. I still have a little bit of it, but it takes time to get rid of old habits."

Jubal, I noticed, has an old habit we need to work on, too: he's afraid of cows, just like his mom, Jewel, used to be. It's interesting how traits like that can be passed between generations. He's a sweet guy, and a perfect fit for Lori in that regard, but he's a bit timid. Much of his time at the ranch this summer has been spent chasing cows around the arena, building his confidence by putting him in a dominant role. I don't want to leave a hole in his foundation that could get Lori hurt.

Her own foundation is stronger now, but she finds it hard to be patient with the slow pace of her recovery. "As a forty-eight-year-old woman, it's frustrating to have days when I don't know how I'm going to get to my car from the cart return in the grocery store parking lot without something to hang on to. It's frustrating to have to ask myself which leg I'm going to lead with in order not to fall. But I think that it's helped me be more compassionate and better at dealing with people who are struggling."

Recently, Lori took a job as the secretary in the special education department of a local junior high school. There are about ninety kids classified as special needs, some of whom were categorized that way at a young age. Sometimes, when their behavior is too disruptive, these kids will be sent to the counselor's office. But they started showing up in Lori's office instead. She'd talk to them, listen to them, and help them complete their class-work. "It's been amazing," she says. "I've found that I kind of like the troubled ones. Because I know how they feel. These kids don't necessarily have mental issues; many of them are very bright. They just don't function well in a regular classroom." Some of them, she knows, come from difficult or traumatic cir-cumstances. They don't have a solid foundation. *Slow to take and quick to give* is a principle Lori has found helpful in this regard.

"I give them what they need, and I take whatever they're able to give. They just want someone to listen to them and not ex-pect too much of them when they're feeling the way they're feeling. There was one kid who, if things weren't going the way he wanted, would get up and pace in the classroom. And the teacher would tell him to sit down. I asked her, If he's not both-ering anyone, can't he just pace for a minute? But she replied that he was distracting the class. So I offered to take him out into the hallway and pace with him for a few minutes there. And then he went back in and sat down." Like Jubal does for her, Lori makes these kids feel understood. "I don't expect more of them than they can do," she says. And because of that, she's able to help them make progress. She knows that it's not about today, it's about the rest of their lives.

CHAPTER EIGHT

If You Deal with an Attitude, You Won't Have to Deal with an Action

Face the simple fact before it comes involved.
Solve the small problem before it becomes big.

—LAO TZU

I F YOU CAN'T FIX HIM, I'm going to have to can him."
This ultimatum was my introduction to James Dean.
He was a big, athletic chestnut thoroughbred whose desperate owner called me one day. A wealthy and accomplished
horsewoman who owned a ranch in Aspen, Colorado, Rita had
already paid good money to several trainers to work with her
horse. She'd been close to giving up when she heard about me
from a friend and decided to give me a shot. I told her to bring
the horse to a clinic I was giving, and I'd see what I could do.

James Dean was well named: this animal had all the mak-
ings of a superstar. His good looks and swagger turned heads
wherever he went. (I confess, I didn't know who James Dean
was before I met that horse, but when Rita described the movie
star to me, straddling a motorcycle with a cigarette hanging out
of the corner of his mouth and a defiant glint in his eye, I could

see why she'd given the horse that name.) You could drive him over jumps without a rider and he'd sail through the air with perfect style. Rita had hoped he'd become a champion jumper. The only problem was, as soon as anyone tried to get on his back, the horse would freak out. He'd rear up so high he'd fall over backward—a terrifying and dangerous habit. Now she, along with every trainer who had tried to help her, was scared of him. When she arrived at the clinic, she'd reached the end of her rope. My ability to fix James Dean would literally mean life or death for this beautiful but unruly animal.

When I looked at the horse, standing on the other side of the pen watching me, he reminded me of myself at a young age. Like a strong-willed kid who'd been given his own way for far too long, he'd grown up without any boundaries. I wasn't scared of him, but I approached him with caution—after all, this rebel without a cause weighed about thirteen hundred pounds and could take me out with one kick. Mostly, though, I felt sorry for him. No one had cared enough to apply some healthy discipline at the time when he needed it most, as a youngster. They probably thought they were loving him. But their brand of love had condemned him to a difficult life—a life full of conflict and struggle.

I often say in my demonstrations: *Discipline without love is abuse, but love without discipline is also abuse.* In fact, I'd argue it's not really love at all.

James Dean, or JD as we called him, proved this point. He'd been petted and praised and indulged, but never taught to respect humans or follow their direction. Now, at four years old, he'd become dangerous, so people kept trying more forceful and painful restraints. In turn, he became more belligerent and disrespectful. It's a cycle that can end up with a perfectly healthy horse being euthanized because he hurts someone. Where's the love in that?

How to Deal with an Attitude

Discipline is part of love. If you don't do it, somebody else is going to have to, down the road, and by then the problem will have gotten worse and the response will be stronger. It's like I tell some parents: If you don't discipline your kids, sooner or later they'll grow up without any respect for rules. They'll disrespect their teachers, and eventually they'll disrespect society, and law enforcement will discipline them instead. They'll end up in jail, angry and resentful at the world, and feeling like the system is unfair. You know what's really unfair? It's unfair that the people tasked with raising them never bothered to draw a line and be consistent about it. How many young people go off the rails because their parents practiced love without discipline?

I know "discipline" is not a popular term these days, but it's essential for a leader who wants to create harmonious partnerships, whether in the herd, the round pen, the workplace, or the family. Many people struggle with this. Some resort to old-fashioned forms of discipline that lack love and border on abuse.

But it seems to me that these days, people are more likely to abandon discipline altogether, believing love alone is enough. Of course, it's a positive thing that we as a society are leaving behind some of the abusive ways we used to treat animals, kids, and people. But oftentimes, I wonder if we've swung too far in the opposite direction and ended up with a different kind of abuse. Many of the horses I've known have proven this to be true.

Striking the right balance of firmness and fairness is never an easy task. It's important to remember: first, do no harm. Don't discipline out of anger or frustration; be as soft as you can but as firm as necessary. Be sensitive to when it's enough—it's easy to do too much. These are skills that we desperately need to develop as humans. Just think how many tragedies in our world might be averted if people were able to be more observant of those around them, spot the signs that spell trouble, and intervene before people get hurt. Among all the lessons I share with visitors who come to the ranch, this one feels particularly urgent to me.

When it comes to horses, the most important lesson I ever learned about discipline is this: if you deal with an attitude, you don't have to deal with an action.

JD had an attitude from the first moment he entered my round pen. He showed the whites of his eyes and tossed his head. As he passed me, he swatted his tail and turned his hip threateningly in my direction. Those are signs of an attitude that can quicky turn into actions like kicking, biting, or striking. My job is to not let it get that far. If you let things get out of hand, it can be devastating, and then you're going to have to pay the price later and go back and fix something. And it will be a lot harder at that point than it would have been to nip it in the bud before it got started.

You never forget the way a horse looked right before he kicked you. If you learn how to read his body language, he'll always tell you what he is going to do *before* he does it. If you're quick enough to deal with the look, you won't have to deal with the kick. Deal with the attitude, and you won't have to deal with the action. That's the power of being observant.

As humans, our problem tends to be that we're caught up in our own private worlds. We don't always pick up on what someone is saying with their eyes, their expression, their posture. We miss the subtle signals, and don't respond until the person acts out in much more visible and destructive ways.

Dealing with an attitude early can short-circuit bigger problems, whether in horses or humans. With JD, I could tell it was going to be hard work because his attitude had been unchallenged for too long by the time I met him. Had the humans in his life found a better balance between love and discipline when he was a colt, he would have been spared much trouble.

The first step was to make it clear right away that I wasn't going to let him bully or intimidate me. When I placed my heavy stock saddle on the horse's back, he threw what we cowboys call a walleyed fit. From the moment I pulled the cinch tight and turned him loose in the round pen, he left the earth, going straight into the air, squealing and snorting. He landed with his head between his legs and his nose to the ground. From there, he jumped again, pirouetting on his hind legs, then back to bucking and bawling.

When a horse bucks, it usually means one of two things: fear or anger. (Occasionally, it can also mean pain, but I was reasonably sure JD wasn't in pain.) As a horse trainer, it's critical to know the difference.

On the surface, anger and fear might look the same, so you've got to read the more subtle body language. If you mistake fear for anger and discipline a horse that's afraid of you, you'll only increase his fear. I don't ever want to punish a horse for being afraid—that's his nature. If you mistake anger for fear and try to love on a horse that's just mad, you'll likely make him worse.

I think this common confusion between anger and fear extends to humans, too, especially young people. Some can look cocky and rebellious and aggressive, but underneath they're just afraid. Those kids need kindness and understanding, not punishment. Then there are other kids that are just plain angry and disrespectful, and all the love and kindness in the world won't help them if you're not willing to draw a firm line. It's tough love they need. Most of us have a gut feeling about what's needed, but sometimes we override it.

In JD's case, it was clear he was bucking out of rage. This wasn't the kind of reaction you see from a terrified horse that thinks it has a predator on its back. This was a straight-up tantrum. JD had only ever worn a light English saddle before, and he resented the heavy stock saddle with its front and back cinches. Therefore, he needed a lesson in humility. Tantrums are not tolerated in my round pen, which I consider my classroom. To establish my authority like the alpha in a herd, I mounted another horse, an older stallion, and entered the ring. JD challenged my horse immediately, charging at us with the whites of his eyes showing and his teeth bared. I countered the charge, waving my flag in his face, and quickly lifted my leg to avoid being kicked as he wheeled away from me. I then continued to drive him around the ring, the way a stallion or lead mare in the wild will drive a subordinate. The message was clear: You're way out of line and need to learn your place. If you need to throw a tantrum, go ahead, but I'm not going to let it work for you.

JD's red coat darkened with sweat, white lather streaked his sides, and his breath came heavy through his flaring nostrils, but I kept him moving until I saw the fight starting to go out of him. Finally, he stopped, and I stopped, too. I saw him lower his head and submit—maybe for the first time ever. He'd dropped the attitude. Immediately, I backed off and let him rest, praising him with a soft, encouraging voice.

Later that same day, I got on and rode JD without incident, and made enough progress to give his owner hope. But she was still too scared to ride him herself, so she asked me to take him back to the ranch for training. JD became part of the family, and I did just what I would have done with any teenager: I put him to work. There's no better cure for an attitude than good old-fashioned hard work! Especially with young horses, it's really important to establish a good work ethic, to get them into a practice of working every day—not all day, but every day. A lot of the problems you have with horses (particularly young ones) is they don't want to work. My young horses work for up to an hour, six days a week, and they get one day off, like we do. And because it's consistent, they aren't resentful, they expect it, and even come to enjoy it, I believe. Every day they do their part.

JD was expected to do his part just like any other horse. That fancy thoroughbred became a humble ranch horse—herding and sorting cattle, roping and doctoring the sick cows, and standing patiently with his saddle on between jobs. It took consistent work and clear boundaries to undo much of the damage done by years of being indulged, but eventually his bad attitude melted away. That strong will became an asset, as he turned out to have incredible endurance and courage. I even started using him to train other unruly colts, driving them around the pen as I had once done with him.

When the time came for JD to depart, I was sad to see him go. He'd become a valued partner to me. But he had a higher calling than ranch work. A few months later, Rita sent me a video of JD at a horse show with a kid on his back, performing a perfect jumping round. We were amazed at how beautiful he looked as he effortlessly cleared the jumps, his mane and tail braided and his chestnut coat shining. He had confidence, without the attitude. He truly commanded attention. I was overwhelmed by feelings of pride in JD, and gratitude to Rita for putting such trust in me. His value, she told me, was more than $100,000.

It's Never Too Late to Try

The worst thing about an attitude is that it's infectious. It can poison the culture of a workplace or playground, and it can turn a home into a battleground. Kids will see a bad attitude as cool and try to imitate it, especially if it goes unchecked. Employees will start to feel resentful and unmotivated if a colleague consistently gets away with acting out. Back when I used to give clinics, I remember how one participant with a bad attitude could turn the day bad for everyone. An attitude needs to be dealt with quickly, clearly, firmly, and decisively.

It's much easier to deal with an attitude early on, but it's never too late to try. I remember one time I was giving a clinic in Georgia. Most of the participants were eager, positive, and engaged, but way in the back I noticed a grizzled old cowboy, chewing tobacco and regarding me with suspicion from under his worn black Stetson. Although he was clearly trying not to be noticed, his attitude was sheer skepticism. Arms crossed, leaning back, his body language was against me. I wondered why he was even there. Could I deal with that attitude, or would it be wiser to just ignore him, as most people seemed to do? I couldn't help but feel he'd showed up at my clinic for a reason. Some part of him wanted to learn, even if he didn't want to be seen doing it.

I decided it was worth a shot. After all, I didn't want his attitude to affect the rest of the clinic. And I just had an intuition

I should try. Dealing with an attitude doesn't always mean being harsh or disciplinary. In this case, I took a different approach. I'd dealt with this kind of pride before and learned that the best course of action is to try to defuse it, not challenge it. I needed to get him working for me, not against me.

"Sir, you look like you know your way around a horse. Can I get you to help me out in here?"

Grudgingly, he came forward and joined me in the ring. By asking for his help, I honored the fact that he was an old hand. Soon, I got him engaged in helping some of the kids. Slowly, he softened. The fight went out of him and I could feel him paying close attention to everything I shared. I hadn't brought my own horse with me that day, since I'd flown in for the clinic, but the old cowboy offered to lend me his brown gelding, which turned out to be a very good horse, and well trained.

Later, I learned the reason for his presence at the clinic. One of his granddaughters was participating, and he hadn't seen her in years because he was estranged from her mother. No wonder he'd seemed uncomfortable at the beginning. He didn't know if he was welcome.

Later, I heard reports that, after the clinic, he had reconnected with his family. There had been forgiveness and reconciliation among three generations—his wife was extremely grateful for the change he had made, enabling them to reconnect with their daughter and granddaughter. Even after decades of resentment and rage over who knows what, that tough old cowboy had been able to drop the attitude. No matter how long you've been on one track, it's never, ever too late to change and start doing something different. It's never too late to humble up and do the right thing and say the right thing.

Bury the Buck

When I work with young horses, I'm on the lookout for a bad attitude from day one, and I don't hesitate to correct it. I know there's nothing to be gained from postponing that confrontation until they're bigger and stronger and more confident. I believe the same applies with people. Like a good horseman, a sensitive leader, coach, or parent is able to read attitudes and anticipate how those might lead to problematic behaviors down the road. A clear but firm correction at the first hint of trouble can save so much struggle later on.

You won't get to see that attitude unless you're willing to put a bit of pressure on the horse when he's young. I don't mind if a colt bucks the first time I put a saddle on him. It's usually a healthy thing. If he needs to buck, that's the time to do it, before you've got a rider up there who can get hurt. If you skirt that kind of confrontation by being too soft on the horse, he doesn't get it out of his system, and sooner or later it will show up when you least expect it. Like the time a couple of weeks ago when one of the gentlest horses in my herd bucked me off with no warning.

I should have known better. I'm more cautious than I used to be about getting on a horse that's likely to buck; at my age the last thing I need are broken bones. But the horse that bucked me off wasn't a young unbroken colt or a wild mustang. It was a horse I'd been working all winter, a bay gelding by the name of Legs. I'd bought him because he seemed so gentle, and he'd lived up to those expectations—until that day.

Legs was "on hot feed," as we say on the ranch, which means he'd been eating the rich, high-protein spring grass. I hadn't worked him for a few weeks, but expecting him to be just like he'd been all winter, I hopped on and rode out to the big round pen. Suddenly, a herd of horses from the neighbor's ranch came galloping across the pasture. Legs's head went up high, his tail flagged out, and I could tell he wanted to run with them. I wasn't worried—this was not an unusual situation. I just started directing his intense energy around the pen.

But then, all of a sudden, he just broke in two and bucked. He really bucked hard. Even as I was hanging on to the saddle horn for dear life, the thought crossed my mind that he might never have really bucked before. It seemed to almost scare him, the rage he was in, which made him buck even harder. I hung in there for a while, but I'm older and slower these days, and eventually I weakened. I bit the dust *hard,* hurting my back. Wincing at the pain, I tried to get up, but thought better of it, and sat there for a minute to catch my air. Looking up at the horse, still bucking around the ring, I wondered what I'd missed. Clearly, I'd taken him for granted because he had always seemed so nice and gentle.

As I thought back over my experience with the horse, I realized that there had been a few warning signs. He was a bit pushy and didn't honor space too well. He'd pin his ears a lot, which is a sign a horse is grumpy. Perhaps the woman who'd started him had never really confronted him or set boundaries in such a way that might have brought out his attitude. Most colts, pretty early in the process of breaking them, will go through a couple of tantrums. If you don't let it work for them, they grow out of it and mature. But maybe this horse had just been loved on, allowed to get his way, and was never pressured enough to bring out his anger.

Now that I'd seen the attitude, I had no choice but to deal with it. I was in no hurry to get back in the saddle and go for round two. I was pretty banged up. But I knew if I limped away and left it at that, Legs would get the message that bucking worked for him. The last thing he remembered would be that he got out of work by bucking me off. Instead, I decided to use an old horseman's technique known as "laying them down." If you've seen the Robert Redford movie *The Horse Whisperer,* you may remember a scene where he does this. It's not a technique I employ very often, but sometimes my instinct tells me that it will help a particular horse. I took Legs into the middle of the arena, the exact spot he had bucked me off, put my rope on his front foot, and then looped it up over the saddle horn. Applying gentle pressure, I got him to first lift the leg, then bow forward on three legs, yielding to the pressure. Eventually, he let out a groan of submission and lay down on his side in the dirt.

Laying down doesn't hurt a horse, but it does humble them. It takes away his natural defenses, leaving him vulnerable and diminished in stature. I'm not talking about throwing a horse to the ground the way the old cowboys sometimes did—this is a slow and careful process that I only do in a safe environment. I'm just dealing with his attitude, between him and me. This is a one-on-one confrontation between the two of us. To reinforce the message, once Legs was lying down, I sat on him. And then I gave him a good talking to. I told him his behavior was unacceptable and wouldn't be tolerated. He could have hurt me bad, and I didn't deserve that. I've treated him right. He's not a green colt; he should be past such a major meltdown over nothing.

Of course, Legs doesn't speak English, but he got the message. My body language backed up my words: I was establishing respect. I didn't beat up on him, but I didn't love on him, either. When I'd said my piece, I sat there for a couple more minutes, feeling the horse relax and his anger subside. He was giving up his will. Some people are afraid of breaking a horse's spirit by insisting he submit. I don't believe you need to break their spirit, but you do need to break the rebellious will that wants to fight.

The next day, I saddled Legs again and took him out to the round pen. Some horsemen would try to "bring out the buck"— provoke the horse in order to confront the problem behavior head-on. I don't do that. To my mind, that's just asking to get bucked off again, and it risks creating a pattern in the horse's head. Instead, I started over, going back to basics, working on any little things that bothered him. I helped him make it through his session without bucking. I didn't even ride him for a few days, just started with groundwork. Then I put some easy rides on him. My goal was for him to realize that he didn't have to buck, day after day, so that I could solidify the good choices and create a positive pattern.

My feeling: when someone (horse or human) messes up, I don't want to emphasize what he did wrong. What I do want to do is slowly increase the pressure, asking a little more of him each day, but staying, as Tom Dorrance used to say, "just this side of trouble." Each day, I'll push that line right up to where I feel like he might want to buck, then back off and make it good for him and let him know that he doesn't have to buck. Each day, that line moves a bit further out, but he moves with it— and he never again has to have that traumatic experience where he gets pushed too far and someone gets hurt (or hurts him). By staying just this side of trouble, I can let him know that it's always better for him if we get along. I'm not going to make life hard on him. I want to build that confidence that he *can* be good. I could bring that buck out if I pushed him too hard, but what good would that do? As Tink would put it, "Build on the good and maybe the bad will just melt away." Or as I like to say, let's bury the buck.

Since this episode, Legs has humbled up a bit and gained some respect. He's a good horse, and I hope that our little meltdown will be not only the first but also the *last* time he bucks someone off.

CHAPTER NINE

You Can Be Bitter or You Can Be Better

Bad things do happen; how I respond to them defines my character and the quality of my life. I can choose to sit in perpetual sadness, immobilized by the gravity of my loss, or I can choose to rise from the pain and treasure the most precious gift I have—life itself.

—WALTER ANDERSON

WHEN I FIRST SAW the bay filly, she was standing ankle-deep in mud and manure, head hanging, ears drooping. Her long mane and tail were matted and tangled, her coat rough and dull. Her muscles were atrophied and every rib showed. She had long hooves, cracked and broken from lack of trimming. She was one of several in a corral full of horses that's known as the "kill pen" at an auction, meaning that they would soon head to the slaughterhouse if someone didn't buy them. Little did I know that this sad-looking filly would change more than I would have thought was possible, and in the process, would change me, too.

I met the filly at a low point in my life, back in the eighties when I was living in California, playing polo and training horses. My first marriage was on the rocks and I was beating myself up for mistakes I'd made with the people and the horses in my life. I needed something to make me feel excited about my life and work again.

The seller at the auction told me the horse was three years old and not even broke to lead—she'd never been touched. She was a "divorce deal"—meaning someone got stuck with her in a divorce and wanted to off-load her quickly. Perhaps she reminded them of an ex they'd now rather forget. Looking at her, I figured it was unlikely anyone would think she was worth much, even for meat. But I was starting to learn how to look for potential—how to see a horse as it could be rather than as it was right now. When I imagined her healthy and fit, three hundred pounds heavier, I saw potential. She was built for speed and stamina. And her eyes—wide-set like a deer's—were not the eyes of a horse that has given up. Despite the hard times she'd fallen upon, there was kindness in her eyes, though they quickly turned glassy and fearful when she felt threatened. Despite everything that had conspired against her in life, I could see that she was still willing. When I got in the pen to take a closer look, and waved a rope to get her going, she trotted out along the fence gracefully. Even in her emaciated condition, she would move her feet quickly. She would *try*. And that is all I had to see to know I could make something out of that horse.

At the trailer gate she spooked, spun around, and raced back down the alley straight at me. I waved her back. Each time she changed directions her hind feet slid up under her as she rolled over her hocks. Within a couple of strides she was galloping full speed the opposite direction. The slick surface had little effect on her. *What an athlete,* I thought, envisioning her on the polo field. After several refusals the filly cautiously stuck her head inside the horse trailer and smelled the floor. One foot then two, gradually three and four, and she was standing in the trailer. Then she spun, jumped out, and ran back toward me. "That's all right, girl," I said. "You take your time. I'm in no hurry. We'll just practice loading and unloading." I wouldn't have put it this way at the time, but I was turning something she was afraid of into a tool to help her learn. If she wanted to get out of the trailer, that was a skill she needed to learn, too. And then she could practice getting in again. Eventually, she went into the trailer and stood quietly inside. I eased the steel gate shut and headed back home.

When my then wife, Locke, looked into the trailer, she raised her eyebrows. "What'd you buy?" I swung open the trailer gate and the bay filly ran out into the round pen. "Looks like a rack of bones."

"She looks pretty rough now, but I think she has potential. The price was right." I wasn't quite sure why, but I just felt like I could make something good of this filly. And I wanted to try.

The next morning, I woke early as the morning light crept up the snow-covered mountain range that rose up from the valley floor. Frogs croaked in the pond and a meadowlark sang its morning song. I hurried out to the horse corrals, eager to work with my new horse.

When I entered the pen the filly flagged her tail in the air, raced to the opposite side of the pen, and crashed into the steel panels. With her chin over the top rail, she weaved back and forth, looking to jump out. Halter in hand, I stepped to the center and began driving her around the pen. Her coat was soon white with lather. She kept looking out at the other horses to provide her some security. "Sweetheart, the answer to your problems isn't out there. Just take a look at me." As she moved around, her inside ear pointed toward me and she gave me a quick glance. I stepped back and away from her toward her favorite place, where the horses were, and then stopped and stood motionless, non-threatening. She slowed to a walk, dropped her nose to the ground as if sniffing the dirt, and licked her lips. "That's it," I said softly. "I'm not going to hurt you."

Tentatively she took a couple of steps toward me, and then I got smaller and less threatening by dropping to one knee. I let her stand quietly and rest. She gradually eased her way closer. On my hands and knees, I inched up within a couple of feet of her nose, but she looked ready to flee, so I withdrew a bit and waited. In about a minute she moved closer to sniff my hat. Soon she was touching my hat, then my shoulder, with her nose. I could feel her warm breath on my neck.

I held out my hand and waited. She slowly put her muzzle on it, and sniffed. Still on my knees, I crawled away a few feet to the side. She followed hesitantly, reaching for me with her head. Gingerly I turned and breathed into her nostrils much like horses do when they meet. Slowly I got to my feet and walked around her. She turned and followed like a dog following its master.

This acceptance and bonding had happened to me before, but this time it overwhelmed me. Perhaps it was because I was feeling so low and so alone at that moment. I was astounded by the love that wrapped around me like a warm blanket. I fell to my knees as tears filled my eyes. The little mare stood next to me with her nose touching my shoulder. As I looked up at her, I saw something of myself—a man beaten down by my own self-criticism and desperate for help. The connection with the filly—her unconditional acceptance—sparked something in me: a flicker of hope.

The next morning, I felt a new energy and couldn't wait to see my little mare; this time she came straightway to greet me. Would she let me pet her? She tensed and wheeled away as I reached out to touch her. "It's okay, girl," I said. "I know you're afraid. We'll try again."

It took only a fraction of the time it had taken the day before for her to turn toward the center of the pen—and without all the sweat. "I'm sorry," I said. "I moved too quickly the first time." Easing my hand toward her shoulder, fingers relaxed and pointed down, I reached out to touch her. She did not run, and I gently swept my hand down her neck, feeling her rough coat and wasted muscles. "That's not so bad, is it? Someday that'll feel good to you." She stood quietly while I rubbed her. Occasionally she reached back and sniffed me for reassurance. When I finished rubbing her, she followed me around. "That's probably enough for today," I said. "Let's end on a good note." For some reason I couldn't think of the right name for her. *No worries,* I thought, *it'll come.*

As the days passed, the filly changed, and so did I. My

approach became softer, less critical, more accepting. After the hundreds of horses I had worked with, why did this one have such a strong effect on me? I wasn't sure, but as I began to think differently, my horses responded by performing better, more willingly. It was more about connection and relationship than methods. Perhaps I was less threatening to them and seemed less like a predator and more like a friend. I learned to appreciate them for what they were instead of trying to force them into what I thought they should be. I noticed and developed their talents and interests. For the first time in my life I understood acceptance. I quit comparing myself to others. Little by little the burden of self-condemnation lifted.

Metamorphosis had transpired and the filly progressed rapidly. She had transformed from a caterpillar into a butterfly. Soon I was riding her. She gained weight, her bay coat became as shiny as a copper penny, and her black mane and tail grew long and glistened in the sun. Her muscles took shape until she looked exactly as I had imagined she would. Then one day I was loping her across the polo field when Locke galloped up beside me. She looked excited. "I have the name for your mare."

"What's that?"

"Milagro," she said. "It's Spanish for 'miracle.'"

The name settled easily on my mind. "That's perfect."

A miracle indeed. It was a name she was already living up to, and she would continue to do so. Only six months after I picked her out of the kill pen, I sold her to a polo player from Wichita, Kansas, for $15,000. She had become more than I had imagined, and she had changed me in ways I could not yet appreciate.

Turn Something Bad
into Something Good

Milagro taught me many lessons, not least of which was that miracles *do* happen. Or, put another way: you can turn almost anything bad into something good. To some extent—though not in all cases—I think the same principle applies in life. Bad things happen to all of us. We can't always control what comes our way, and sometimes we just have to bear the pain of loss or hurt or betrayal until time heals the wound. But when I find myself in the midst of a challenge or a setback, I always try to at least consider the question: Can I use this for good? Is there the seed of a miracle hidden in the darkness?

When I come up against an issue with a horse—something he doesn't like or something he is afraid of—rather than punishing him, I use the "bad" thing to create pressure and teach him new skills. It might be a flapping tarp or a water hose. It might be the frightening applause of the audience around the pen. Whatever he reacts negatively to, I can use that trigger to get his feet moving so he becomes more supple and responsive. And I try to live my life that way as well. I believe that many bad things can be used for good. It all depends on your attitude.

I'm not just talking about putting a positive spin on things, or denying life's challenges and hardships. I've had plenty of moments in my life where I felt like everything was working against me and I couldn't see the way out. And some things are just plain hard and painful. But I've learned that even in our darkest moments, we do have a choice about how we react. There's always a possibility of something brighter on the other side, and we sometimes find goodness in the most unexpected places.

I think this philosophy is one of the reasons I often go to the kill pen at horse sales, like I did the day I found Milagro. This is where horses end up when the humans in their lives have given up on them or can't care for them anymore. They're basically throwaways—unwanted horses that will go for meat unless someone decides to give them a chance. They've been written off as too difficult, too broken down, too wild, or just too much of a burden. I've always been drawn to these horses— partly for the challenge and partly because I can buy them cheap, put them on a new track, and sell them for a handsome profit. That's the name of the game: buy low, sell high. You can't save them all—I know that, having learned it the hard way. But I've discovered great satisfaction in giving these animals a new shot at a good life. One man's trash is another man's treasure, as they say. These horses have become precious to me, and they've taught me some of life's most important lessons.

When life deals me a tough hand and I find myself wanting to get angry or feel like a victim, I think about horses like Milagro. They've been through all kinds of difficult, frightening situations, but their spirits haven't been broken. They're still willing to try, and in some cases they undergo remarkable transformations. It puts me in mind of something my mother once said to me at a low point in my life—something that's stuck with me for decades: "You can be bitter or you can be better."

"It's Easy to Be Bitter, but It's Hard to Live That Way"

If anyone has a reason to be bitter, it's my friend Steven Millward. He's paralyzed, and has been that way for decades, living his life confined to a motorized wheelchair. But Steven is one of the most positive and optimistic people I've ever met. "It's easy to be bitter," he once told me, "but it's hard to live that way."

Before we got to know each other, I remember seeing Steven in that chair at local rodeos. He'd always be somewhere near the bucking-horse chute, talking to the young riders, encouraging them, giving advice. He had an energy and enthusiasm that seemed at odds with his situation. I sometimes wondered what his story was, but I didn't find out for a few years.

One summer, I was looking for colts to use in our demonstrations, and I noticed that there were some nice young horses in the pasture right across the highway. When I inquired about who owned them, it turned out they were Steven's. Thinking that maybe he could use some help starting them, and in return I would get some young horses for my demonstrations, I called him up. He quickly agreed to my proposal. As I got to know

Steven, and heard his story, he soon became a friend, and one of my heroes.

Steven had been just a few weeks away from his nineteenth birthday when he and some friends drove out to a rodeo in Baker, Montana. Born and raised in Jackson, he had grown up with horses and cattle and loved to compete in team roping, calf roping, and especially in bronc riding.

That day, he'd entered the saddle bronc competition. The ride started out like countless others. Steven climbed the fence above the chute containing the horse, and he lowered himself carefully into the saddle. He felt the horse quivering beneath him. He wrapped the frayed rope securely around his calloused hand, thrust his feet forward in the stirrups, and leaned back, ready for the jump. The gate swung open, the crowd roared, and the horse exploded into a convulsion of bucking. For a few seconds, Steven went with him, matching his rhythm like a surfer riding a big wave. And then he was flying through the air, and the first thing to hit the ground was his head.

The next thing he remembers is the painted face of the rodeo clown swimming into focus above him. He couldn't breathe.

"You're all right, son. You just got the wind knocked out of you. Let's get you on your feet."

It took everything he had, but Steven managed to gasp out three words: "Don't . . . move . . . me."

"I knew," he says, "the minute it happened. You don't mistake it when you break your neck."

As he lay there in the dirt, somewhere above him he heard a familiar voice and knew that his paramedic-trained father would take care of everything. "So I just kind of checked out," he recalls. "My peace in life came at that moment. I was sure this was the end."

He woke up in the ambulance on the way to the hospital. His first thought? "Why won't they turn the damn sirens off?" It felt like his head was going to explode. But in the midst of that agonizing ride, he received a clear message. "It was not my time. I think God placed a sense of peace in my heart, assuring me that I had plenty more to offer in life."

I've heard it said that a cowboy is a man with guts and a horse. Well, Steven has both. He has more guts than the most daredevil bronc rider. Many people in his situation might never have wanted to look at a horse again, but not this man. He may not be able to ride anymore, but he's still a cowboy. "It's how I was made," he says. "It's in my DNA. It's as much a part of me as having brown hair." In fact, not long after he got home to Jackson after months of "getting pieced back together" at a Denver hospital, he went to a horse auction, just fifty miles from the site of his accident, and bought himself a horse. A quiet old retired horse? Not a chance. He bought a bucking-horse stallion.

Despite being confined to his wheelchair, unable to move, Steven's plan was to raise bucking horses with his uncle. "Horses were one way of resurrecting my life back to some semblance of normality," he explains. A smile softens his voice as he remembers. "That bucking-horse stud was dog-gentle. He was really, really nice." Steven started to just hang out with the horses, wheeling his motorized chair out into the pasture. "I've learned so much more about horses just watching them in the corrals than I ever did riding them," he says. He's become fascinated by their body language—their mouths, their ears, their eyes, the way they stand. "You can learn so much from watching horses, and not just about horses. When you start relating it to the human experience, you see that there's something of everybody in that corral."

Steven has turned the bad into good more than anyone I've ever met. I've never once seen him express bitterness or regret. He says that from the moment he woke up in that ambulance, he's never felt any animosity about what happened—not even toward the horse that hurt him. "He was just doing his job!" He even jokes that "it cost me a hundred and fifty bucks to break my neck," referring to his rodeo entry fees. With a more serious tone, he told me once, "I wouldn't be the man I am today if this hadn't happened to me." The accident, he says, was "a bump in the road. It's something I'll overcome." At first, he was sure that overcoming it would mean walking again, but it slowly became clear that wasn't going to happen for him. Now he's adjusted to overcoming it in other ways. "I've overcome a great deal of the paralysis," he says. "I couldn't move anything at first. Now I've got most of my feeling back. I can move my right arm pretty good." He's also learned to operate a computer with his voice.

Steven is one of the most inspiring people I know. It's a great honor for me to get to be his hands and feet when it comes to training his colts. These days, however, he's had less time for his beloved horses. He's spending many of his days far from the wide-open Wyoming spaces that he calls home. Closely shadowed by his devoted dog, Walter, he maneuvers his wheel-chair around a small student-housing unit in Laramie, Wyo-ming, where he's attending law school—getting his JD as well as a master's in environmental and natural resources. He's got two more years to go. "I figured it was probably time for me to get my education," he says.

When asked what he plans to do once he graduates, he's open-minded. "I've learned," he reflects without a hint of bitter-ness, "not to put all my eggs in one basket. So, let's see where life takes me." Knowing Steven, I have no doubt it will keep getting better.

CHAPTER TEN

Don't Be Afraid to Move Your Feet

When you lose, don't lose the lesson.

—COWBOY SAYING

W HO'S READY to catch some horses?"

The executives standing around the corral didn't look ready at all. This was not surprising—after all, these folks worked for a tech company and weren't exactly accustomed to handling large animals. Their expressions ranged from excitement to discomfort to fear.

We were about to begin a new exercise: each individual would enter the corral and try to put a halter on a horse. They'd probably have appreciated a few pointers first—which way up the halter goes, which end of the horse is the danger zone, that kind of thing. But in talking with CeCe Morken, the leader whose team I was working with that day, we'd agreed that I wouldn't give people any instructions. CeCe wanted her team to figure it out for themselves. More than that, she wanted them to fail.

This was the fourth time I'd met CeCe, then executive vice

president of Intuit's Strategic Partner Group. The first time, she'd been part of a group of leaders who'd come up to a Montana dude ranch for an award trip. They'd brought me in to do a demonstration. CeCe clearly loved the lessons and took them to heart. She struck me as a deeply thoughtful and empathetic leader. Not long after, she'd invited me down to the company's offices in Fort Worth for another session. Now she'd brought her team to the ranch for an intensive day of exercises.

We don't get to do this kind of in-depth work with every group, but I love it when people choose to not just watch me train a horse but actually get in the pen themselves and experience it firsthand. The philosophy comes alive in a whole new way when you have to put it into practice. CeCe and I had worked together on a plan for the day, with a series of exercises designed to build trust among the team.

One of the principles that had really stuck with CeCe from our earlier encounters was the idea that mistakes and failures are essential to learning. "We're trying to shift our culture to be one that doesn't just reward success, but rewards people for being willing to take risks, even if they fail," she told me. "We're trying to let people have a little more rope, knowing that if they trip it's not such a big deal, they learn better that way. Failure can lead to learning, and we want people to be 'learn-it-alls' instead of 'know-it-alls.'"

CeCe knew that it's not enough to just tell people it's okay to make mistakes or to fail. The leader needs to model that herself—which is why she was willing to be one of the first to try her hand at catching a horse that day. If people feel judged or ridiculed when they make mistakes, they'll be afraid to try, even if the leader is saying it's okay. That's why CeCe wanted her team to work hands-on with the horses themselves, and to do so in front of their peers.

"I want people to get comfortable being in situations that they haven't been in before, because learning is a really big priority for me," she told me as we stood watching the horses in the corral.

Well, I thought, looking around at the group of executives standing awkwardly along the fence, *they are certainly going to do some learning today—and probably some failing as well.* I unlocked the corral gate, held up a rope halter, and asked, "Who wants to go first?"

The executives were divided into teams. One person from each team was to go into the corral, pick a horse from the herd, halter it, and move it to a pen. The other team members were allowed to give suggestions from the fence. The team that moved all their horses first and were ready to go to work would be the winners.

The first volunteers stepped up and took the halters. I watched a woman enter the corral. She started snapping her fingers and clucking at the horse—a good way to convince him to move off rather than stand still and be caught, which is exactly what he did. The big, confident-looking guy from the other team took a different approach. He walked straight toward a horse's face, holding the halter up in both hands as if he expected the horse to just stick his nose in. The horse, confused and a little offended by this approach, turned his head and ambled off. Another guy crouched down in the dirt the way you might do with a dog, calling to the horse: "Come here, good boy. Here, here." The horse didn't move.

At first, the rest of the team members along the fence laughed at the mishaps of their colleagues. But pretty soon, people stopped laughing and started to offer suggestions. Once a few of them had tried their hand at catching a horse, they realized it wasn't as easy as they thought. The teams started to work together, and the person taking a turn in the corral didn't feel so exposed and foolish. They figured out how to approach the horses from one side, staying within their natural field of vision. They learned how to carry the halter low, so as not to spook the horse, and then slowly slip it up over the nose and knot it. Finally, one team burst out cheering as they successfully haltered their last horse and moved him into the pen. But rather than take a break and celebrate, the winning team stayed by the fence. One last horse was resisting all attempts at capture. So, competition forgotten, everyone—the winners and the rest—started throwing out suggestions and encouraging the final team member who was struggling to halter her horse. With their support, she, too, finished the task at hand.

If He's Turning, He's Learning

When a horse makes a mistake or fails a test because he's afraid or unsure, I don't punish him for the mistake—if I did, he'd associate that mistake with the punishment and be less likely to want to try again. The last thing I want is for him to freeze up in fear of being corrected. I want him to keep moving his feet, to try again, to search for the answer, and to keep searching.

Let's say I'm trying to get him to step on a large orange tarp. It's a scary, unfamiliar object that rustles in the wind. He's loose in the round pen, so I'm giving him the freedom to choose. I'm not dragging him onto the tarp or forcing him to stay there. But I am making the right thing easy and the wrong thing difficult. I'm putting pressure on him with my flag—making him move faster any time he's moving away from the tarp and releasing the pressure when he approaches it. Nevertheless, he balks, snorting, and spins away from the unfamiliar object. Some horse trainers might punish him for making that wrong choice. They might respond to his failure by trying to drive him across against his will.

I won't do that. But neither will I just give up. Instead, I work him back and forth in front of it, keeping him turning toward his fear but allowing him to move away when he's too troubled by it, then turn back again after a few steps. In the process, he's learning to be handy and quicker on his feet. If he's trying, I don't push harder—that's the time to release. It's okay for him to be afraid, but what's important is that he keeps working at facing his fear—turning toward it again and again—until he overcomes it. If he's turning, he's learning.

I've seen some of the best horses and the best people in my life demonstrate the willingness to keep turning, and learning. They know they don't have to get things right on the first try, and they're not afraid to look foolish. They're able to keep moving, try something different, approach the problem from a different angle, try again.

We all make mistakes. Failures are part of life, and they're essential to learning and growth. Failure just means you figured out what doesn't work. When a young horse is being trained, he'll make plenty of mistakes. That's part of his journey. By allowing him to search and make choices for himself, I encourage him to figure things out. Sooner or later, he learns that it doesn't work to avoid the tarp, or the river crossing, or the road that leads away from the barn.

I look at it this way: as long as the horse is willing to move his feet, he's heading in the right direction. By moving and taking chances, he is either learning what is right or learning what is not right. Either way, it's progress.

If you never fail or make mistakes, you're playing it so safe you're hardly living at all. It's like they say, if you haven't fallen off a horse, then you haven't been riding long enough. People and horses often get stuck because they don't want to make mistakes. They stop moving their feet, and they stop moving toward their destiny. In my experience, there are two reasons for this: either they're too scared or they're too proud.

Pride and fear might seem like very different things, but they have the same end result: you stop moving, stop learning, and stop growing. Pride says, "I don't need to move." Fear says, "I'm afraid to move." If a horse won't move his feet, I can't teach him. I want a horse that's willing to keep moving—they're easier to train that way. As Ray Hunt used to say, "If you want a horse that won't move, get a sawhorse!" It takes courage and humility to try new things, make mistakes, and not give up. If we don't feel the freedom to fail, we'll never try. If we don't try, we'll never make progress.

The fear of failure can keep you from moving forward and cause you to miss a lot of opportunities. Growing up, I saw this happen to my dad. Being a child of the Depression and living through such hard times created a deep-seated fear that he never got over. My dad had several opportunities to buy real estate that would have made him a wealthy man. He even knew it at the time, but just couldn't get past the fear of making a mistake. I remember him struggling over the decisions and desperately wanting to step out and take the risk, but he always talked himself out of it. Like so many horses I've worked with, he became paralyzed by fear and afraid to move. Looking back, I can see that each investment would have been a good one.

This philosophy of allowing the horse to explore on his own terms, making mistakes and learning from them, has had a profound effect on my own life. Now when I fail I don't take it quite as hard, and I try to find the lesson behind it. Some mistakes and failures are small and inconsequential. Others are big and life-altering. I've made plenty of both types, and I'm grateful for them all. Like the horses I've worked with, I've learned to move my feet even when paralyzed by fear, shame, or embarrassment. Along the way, I've come to understand that failure is essential to progress. I often tell myself, "I am going to make mistakes and that's okay. That's how I learn. I give myself permission to fail. I refuse to beat myself up for it and I won't allow anyone else to do so, either."

I also remember something my dear friend Jeremy Morris, whose story I shared in chapter 1, said to me recently. "Failure isn't final." Jeremy made some pretty bad mistakes, and he had many moments where he felt like he'd completely failed. What he realized, he told me, is that "somehow, in our society, we've convinced ourselves that failure is final. We're terrified to make mistakes, and when we do we feel so much shame that we stop trying. But failure isn't final. You can always come back and get on a new track." In Jeremy's story, as in my own, this has been proven again and again. I am still amazed at how life tends to work out if we listen to our hearts and have the faith to keep moving our feet.

Watch, Do, Reflect

I kept working with CeCe Morken's group of leaders at the ranch that afternoon. Following the halter experiment, we progressed to an exercise where the goal was to get a loose horse to "join up" and follow a person in the round pen. Again, the executives had to go in one at a time. They were given a flag to drive the horse, but no rope to compel her to follow. How would they lead?

It was fascinating to see how some people tried to befriend and cajole the horse, while others tried to push and control her.

Neither approach worked. Eventually, they learned to first drive the horse away, establishing respect and making her work hard. Then, once she began to turn her head toward them, they needed to be quick to reward that movement in their direction by releasing the pressure. *Honor the slightest change and the smallest try.* They figured out which body language was threatening to the horse and which was reassuring and inviting. CeCe shared with me later that many people had aha moments as a result of this exercise, realizing that the way they led their teams was very similar to the ways they tried to lead the horse. It doesn't work to just try to be everyone's friend. But neither does it work to just boss people around.

Again, I kept quiet through most of the exercise, not offering instructions but just staying in the pen to make sure no one got hurt. People need the freedom to fail without some so-called expert coming in and taking over. When you know how to do something, it's always tempting to micromanage—to step in and take over a task when you see someone struggling. Sometimes when we do this, we mean well—we want to prevent the person from failing or suffering an embarrassment. Or perhaps we just want to stop them from doing damage. But when a leader does this, the message it sends is that the leader doesn't trust their people and that failure is not acceptable. In turn, people become hard on themselves when they *do* make a mistake. A wise leader has to be sensitive to this. You have to weigh up the potential damage against what could be gained.

We once had a wonderful ranch hand named Keith, but when he first arrived he was clumsy and made plenty of mistakes and missteps. It's one thing to do that when you're standing on the ground, it's quite another when you're driving a backhoe. I remember hearing him inside the barn, bumping that thing into stalls. Every part of me wanted to run in there and take over, or at least stand there so he knew I was watching. But I soon realized that having me overseeing him made him more nervous and more likely to get things wrong. So I stayed out of there, allowing him to figure it out. Soon, the banging stopped and Keith's confidence grew enormously. Keith went on to work for us for nine more years, and became one of the most productive and loyal employees we've ever had.

If we're afraid of failing because we know from experience that when we do our boss will take over, sooner or later we'll just stop trying. And when we stop trying, we stop learning and growing. As another great leader we've worked with, Boot Barn CEO Jim Conroy, puts it, "If a CEO yells, people freeze. Give them a safe space to think clearly. If you pounce on their back, they'll never take a risk again and you'll be micromanaging them forever."*

CeCe had given the design of the program for her team a lot of thought. She wanted people to try things for themselves, fail, try again, and also to reflect on what they learned. Too often, as we go about our busy lives, we don't pause to consider the lessons we're encountering. When we make a mistake or stumble,

---

* Jeanne Sahadi, "What Executives Can Learn from a Horse," CNN Business, August 8, 2019, https://www.cnn.com/2019/08/29/success/executives-horses/index.html.

our main concern is getting back on our feet and dusting ourselves off quickly, hoping nobody noticed. We might learn more if we took a moment to just sit there in the dirt and think about how we ended up there. Learning can turn a failure into a success.

To encourage reflection and learning, CeCe's team was given leather-bound notebooks, which we had them brand with a branding iron. Time was built into the day for people to think and write, as well as gathering around the campfire at the end of the day where they could share and discuss. James Helms, who was the then VP of design, says that the design of the day was itself a powerful lesson. "Watch, do, reflect," he says. "If you don't know what you're doing, watch somebody do it, then try it yourself. And then be intentional about capturing the things that you learned."

When I asked CeCe some months later what her team had taken away from that day, she summed it up in two words: humility and trust. "At first," she said, "when you go into that ring, it's so intimidating that everybody else is watching you. And you know the horse may make a fool of you. It may go the opposite direction and embarrass you." But when people saw that their fellow team members weren't laughing at them, it completely changed the game. "What you end up seeing is that your team is actually encouraging you, and they respect the fact that you went into the ring." This created a new bond of trust among them. "They learned that it's okay for them to show up as who they are. Their colleagues have their back." This feeling has translated back into the office. "If they feel vulnerable, because they're about to launch a new product, or because they said they were going to deliver something and now realize they can't, they know it's okay to ask for help."

I was amazed how much the executives had gotten out of those simple exercises. They'd taken away lessons I wouldn't have anticipated—in fact, I felt like I was learning from their reflections.

Helms remembers how being in such an unfamiliar setting had a leveling effect on the team. No one was an expert when it came to horses. "We had an awful lot of city slickers, so to speak. It put people into an uncomfortable place. And that sense of discomfort really drove the concepts home. There's no better way to put yourself in a position to learn than to be very uncomfortable. And there are few places that make you feel more vulnerable than either standing next to or sitting on top of a thousand-pound animal. It was like we had permission to be humbly bad at it."

He also reflected on how valuable the experience was for folks who were more comfortable dealing with predictable, controllable numbers and spreadsheets than unpredictable, unrestrained animals. "They can do the math," as he put it, "but when you've got people that are accustomed to looking at Excel spreadsheets, they need to think differently in order to manage a team." Working with the horses, they learned to focus on building relationships and positive energy.

CeCe later told me that one team member was so encouraged by this experience that she decided to change jobs—

shifting from a technical role to a business development role, an area she'd never worked in before. She'd started the day at the ranch terrified, and she'd ended it feeling confident and energized. "It showed me that there are things I can do that I didn't think I could," the woman said to CeCe.

Another member of the team, Rajneesh Gupta, the then VP and chief customer care officer, was struck by how the horses reflected back what they sensed from the people. "Human beings are pretty good at hiding their feedback. But with animals, you get the feedback right away through their reactions," he says. "The horse knows what is a safe space. The same is true in an organization. You can try to fake certain things, but team members know when you truly care for them. It taught me the power of being a genuine, honest person. Leadership is not about forcing others to do things you want them to do; it's about having space and humility so that others let you lead them."

For the final exercise of the day with CeCe's team, we had all the executives mounted up on their horses. They'd been riding in the arena for a while, learning the basic skills for communicating with their horses, directing them, starting and stopping. Now I mounted Freckles, rode over, and opened the gate.

"Let's go move some cattle," I said, pointing toward the open pasture. They looked surprised and a little apprehensive about leaving the safety of the corral. But as they gathered up the reins and followed me, mostly they seemed game for a new challenge—and no doubt for some new lessons along the way.

There's Little Growth in the Comfort Zone

It's been my experience that some of the greatest lessons come from discomfort. I've heard it said that there's little growth in the comfort zone and little comfort in the growth zone, and I believe that to be true. We may not enjoy it at the time, and we might not always choose that situation if given another option, but when we look back, we can see how much learning came out of it. It's one of the paradoxes of life. Sometimes you look back at a mistake or a failure and wish you'd done something different. There are mistakes I've made that I'd give anything to be able to go back and undo. But at the same time, I am grateful for the learning. Out of some of my most tragic mistakes, I've learned lessons I'll never forget or regret.

Don't be afraid to move your feet. It seems like a simple idea, but when we're in the middle of feeling scared, ashamed, or embarrassed, it's easy to forget. If you don't move your feet, you may be less likely to make mistakes, but you won't be going anywhere, either, and you won't be learning anything.

It's a lesson I've tried to share not only with the horses but with Jane's and my children, too. Luke, Jane's oldest son, finds the notion of embracing risks, mistakes, and failures to be life-changing. "When you have tough breaks in life," he says, "it can feel like the best strategy is to play it safe—to not take the risk of getting hurt again. But that can also lead to a place where you stop growing, stop taking chances, and stop developing, so you miss out on a lot of the good stuff as well."

Luke had plenty of tough breaks early in his life. Living through two divorces, multiple moves, and a devastating house fire that destroyed everything the family owned, he was no stranger to loss when I showed up on the scene. So it was hardly surprising that he was a guarded young man who was hesitant to put his faith in yet another father figure. As he puts it, "After having so many things go wrong, I just wanted to be safe. Plus, I felt like I was the only security net for my mother and brother. I didn't have the luxury of making mistakes."

Over time, however, Luke began to trust and take chances again—and he says it was due in no small part to seeing how the horses learned to keep moving their feet and working through things. "I started to allow myself to reach out on the risk spectrum, to try for things that seemed out of my reach. And I told myself, 'If it doesn't work out, you can just allow yourself to be okay with failure or setbacks being a part of growth.'"

It's an attitude that's taken Luke all the way from Wyoming to Harvard, where he was the first graduate of Jackson Hole High School to ever be accepted—and with a good scholarship. He went on to build a career at some of Wall Street's most prestigious financial firms, and is constantly pursuing new entrepreneurial ventures.

"I just kept moving my feet, stepping outside my comfort zone, and then one day I looked back and I was amazed at how far I went," he reflects. "If you allow fear to freeze you, it creates a habit. When you're willing to take chances, the opposite can become a habit, too. I don't know that it ever gets easy, because there's always something that's going to scare you in life. But to me, that's a good sign. If life's not a little scary, maybe you're just not taking enough chances. It's like the old cowboy saying, 'If you haven't fallen off a horse yet, you're not riding hard enough.'"

New Pastures, New Challenges

When CeCe Morken left the ranch with her team, she had little sense of what new pastures might await her just over the horizon. But little more than a year later, she would find herself in a completely new role at a new company, navigating unprecedented challenges and changes. In early 2020, she left Intuit to join Headspace Inc., a meditation app developer with millions of users and a big mission: to improve the health and happiness of the world. Just weeks before she officially stepped into her new role as COO, the health and happiness of the world took a dramatic turn with the advent of the COVID-19 pandemic. On top of the learning curve one would expect in a new role, she found herself confronting wholly unexpected challenges, like how to lead her new team virtually; how to support team members working remotely during this extraordinarily difficult year; and how to use the company's technology to help people and communities weather the mental health impacts of the pandemic. Plus, with concerns around social justice coming to the forefront in workplaces across America, she, like many leaders, was plunged into uncomfortable yet essential conversations. The lessons she'd learned at the ranch—*Don't be afraid to move your feet; If you're afraid to make a mistake you'll never learn; Failure just means you figured out how not to do it*—took on a deeper meaning.

"In the conversation about social justice," she says, "I've had to embrace the vulnerability of listening to someone else's experience and admitting, 'I didn't know all that.' I've had to stand up in front of an organization and say, 'I need to do better.' And I've known I won't always find the right words, and I'll make mistakes, but I want to learn." This kind of vulnerability has deepened her sense of the company's mission as well, and she's become passionate about creating space for people to talk about sensitive issues around mental health in the workplace—to admit when they're struggling, when they're overwhelmed, or when they need more space, and to support each other in trying to do better, just as her team back at the ranch supported each other in the unfamiliar business of haltering horses.

Only six months after she joined Headspace, CeCe was promoted to CEO. And as soon as circumstances allow, she's planning to bring her new team up to the ranch for a day of learning, failing, and learning some more. "Working with horses is a great equalizer," she says. "In any team, you have different strengths and capabilities; gifts and shadows. In a business context, sometimes certain people show up with a really big presence—they're articulate and extroverted. Others might get overshadowed because they're more introverted. But at the ranch, it's a whole new playing field because everyone's learning something new and they get to appreciate each other in a different way. Everyone's learning servant leadership. Everyone's learning humility. Everyone has to earn the respect of the horse before the horse will ever do something for them."

I'm looking forward to her visit, too. When leaders like CeCe come to me to learn, I learn just as much from them. That's the beauty of this work and this life: we're all turning, and learning, together.

CHAPTER ELEVEN

Every Horse Needs a Purpose

≋

What man actually needs is not a tensionless state but rather the striving and struggling for some goal worthy of him. What he needs is not the discharge of tension at any cost, but the call of a potential meaning waiting to be fulfilled by him.

—Viktor E. Frankl,
Man's Search for Meaning

I COULD HEAR THE mustangs before I saw them, jostling and banging against the high fences of the small corral. The smell of their sweat and fear hung in the frigid air. It was more than thirty below on a dark January day, and for a brief moment I wondered what had possessed me to drive to Montana in the middle of winter to break a bunch of wild horses. But the next moment, I remembered why I was there, and all doubts vanished. I pulled my hat a little lower against the icy wind and walked across the yard, eager to meet my host.

Micah Fink towered above me—bearded, tattooed, and bundled up against the cold. He had a firm handshake and a warm smile. A former Navy SEAL, Micah is the founder of the nonprofit Heroes and Horses. Since 2013, they've been offering a unique program that takes veterans out into the wilderness on horseback, teaching them survival skills and helping them reconnect with a sense of purpose. A few years after he launched the program, Micah realized he needed more horses if he was to serve the increasing number of applicants. And he couldn't afford to buy gentle, well-trained mounts. So he came up with a creative idea. He knew that there were tens of thousands of mustangs just standing around in Bureau of Land Management holding facilities—a problem the federal government didn't know how to solve. Micah saw a parallel between the plight of these horses and the plight of many veterans. Both lacked a sense of purpose and place in our world. Both were tough, brave, and resilient, but both were suffering. Why not adopt some wild horses to partner with the veterans in his program?

His plan: he could train the horses the same way he helped the veterans—through "covering country." He envisioned taking the mustangs on a five-hundred-mile journey through the New Mexico and Arizona wilderness and making a documentary about the whole thing, so that more people could learn about what he calls "the story of the unpurposed horse and the unpurposed human being." Before he could set out, however, the mustangs needed to be gentled enough to carry a rider or a pack. Which was where I came in. Along with two other trainers, I'd come to Montana in January 2017 to help Micah and his team prepare for their epic journey.

Each trainer was partnered with a member of the Heroes and Horses team. I was assigned to Micah. Together, we went over to the corral to pick out the horse he would train and ride. More than a dozen mustangs crowded against the opposite fence, crashing into each other and the metal panels in their desperation to get as far away from us as possible. They were a hardy bunch, with shaggy coats, battle scars, and fierce, unbroken spirits. These horses had lived most of their lives running wild in the Nevada desert before being rounded up and spending the last few months in an Oregon holding facility. The ones Micah had chosen were between two and four years old—mature enough to carry a rider but not so old they'd become untrainable.

Taking in my new friend's six-foot-four muscled frame, I pointed to the biggest horse in the herd—a brawny chestnut with a tangled flaxen mane and tail and a crooked white stripe down his face.

"This guy looks like a fit. He's got the bones to carry you."

Micah nodded, signaling a willingness to go with whatever I suggested. I was surprised by his easy attitude. This man had led troops into combat. He'd stared down death and attempted missions I couldn't even imagine. He struck me as a very determined person, yet he seemed humble and eager to learn. I was looking forward to working with him—and getting to know his story.

Pressure Uncovers Purpose

Micah has quite a tale to tell, and it starts in an unusual place: up a telephone pole in Queens, New York. He and a friend had a company that installed high-speed internet cables, which is why he was twenty feet off the ground one September morning when he looked across at the downtown skyline and saw a giant plume of smoke. Micah and his buddy shimmied down that pole, jumped in his car, and drove straight toward the smoke. They parked about a mile from downtown and started running. Crowds of dust-covered people ran past them, headed in the other direction. Struggling to breathe, the two men ripped the sleeves off their shirts to create makeshift dust masks and began to scramble over the wreckage of the Twin Towers, searching for survivors. Micah saw horrors that day that he would never forget. When Tower 7 fell, he narrowly avoided being buried in the rubble.

Finally, as the sun was rising on September 12, 2001, the two young men staggered away from Ground Zero and made their way to the Hudson River. They found an upturned bagel cart and scavenged some breakfast. Micah's friend turned to him and asked, "What are we gonna do?"

"I had a choice to make in that moment," Micah says. "Either I accept this or I don't. . . . I was nobody special—just a small-town kid from upstate New York who played drums in a ska band and climbed telephone poles for a living. But that morning I decided I was doing something different."* Sitting there, covered in dust and dirt and overcome by the magnitude of what he'd just witnessed, he made a life-changing decision: he would join the military. He was just twenty-one years old.

---

* Micah Fink, "The Superpower in You," TEDxBozeman, https://www.ted .com/talks/micah_fink_the_superpower_in_you.

He completed the grueling training program to become a Navy SEAL, and later a paramilitary defense contractor. All in all, he would serve thirteen combat tours and spend more than 1,100 days in combat zones over the next four years. He jumped out of planes, piloted submarines, and risked his life countless times. But he says the greatest challenge he faced was coming home.

Like so many veterans, he felt lost. "When I was deployed, I just wanted to be home, but when I was home, I wanted to go back out there." He had a good home life, but combat had changed him, irrevocably, and he didn't know how to fit in anymore. The disconnect was too extreme. "One day I'm tip of the spear Special Operations combat unit; the next day I'm at Whole Foods Market with Cheddar Bunnies and a head of lettuce," he says. "I couldn't connect. It makes you feel isolated and alone."*

Like so many of his fellow veterans, Micah was diagnosed with PTSD. But his instincts told him not to take the meds he was prescribed by a grad student in a white coat at the VA hospital. Instead, he began to seek out challenges, like a six-week trip up the Amazon River in a canoe. Out there in the jungle, accompanied only by a guide who didn't speak English, Micah felt more like himself again. He didn't have time to think about anything other than the moment-to-moment business of surviving. It was then that he began to realize the value of pressure and intensity. Under pressure, we learn who we are. Pressure "peels back the layers," as he puts it, "taking us back to the

---

* Fink, "The Superpower in You."

basics of what it means to be human and what it means to be ourselves."

Back home, Micah began learning about the veteran community. What he discovered shocked him—the homelessness, joblessness, addiction, and suicide rates were just staggering. "These once-great warriors were now popping pills and hiding in their houses waiting for their next check to come to the mailbox," he says.* Tens of thousands of organizations existed to support veterans, and billions of dollars was poured into programs. But the problem seemed to be getting worse. "We have gotten to a place where we've helped people to death, rather than teaching people how to help themselves." Not wanting to get caught in what he describes as "an addiction cycle, where you fall in love with the identity of a psychological condition," in 2013 he packed up everything he owned and moved with his family to Montana.

On a backpacking trip in the wilderness, Micah met a group of cowboys and was drawn to their lifestyle. They introduced him to horses, and even though he was "kicked, bucked off, dragged, and stomped on," he was also hooked. "It was through these obstacles that I began to take ownership of my life again and these horses became a mirror, reflecting my soul, showing me that the problems in my life were caused by me not embracing the struggles. Things became easier as I began to take ownership of my choices."†

---

* Fink, "The Superpower in You."
† Fink, "The Superpower in You."

It was out of these experiences that Heroes and Horses was born. "Sometimes the only way that you can find your own way is by helping somebody else find theirs," Micah says. He recognized that horses can be a powerful tool for helping veterans reconnect with themselves and rediscover a sense of purpose. In fact, he jokes that when people ask him how many therapists he has on staff, his answer is sixty-two—because that's how many horses he has. Why horses? Because, as I shared in the opening chapter of this book, horses never lie. Micah explains it this way: "Horses have evolved to be able to intuitively sense a predator's intentions, and they can sense them at very great distances. So when an individual works with a horse, that animal is going to sense the person's true intentions—even if they're not visibly presented on the outside—and have a reactionary behavior. In this way, the horse becomes a reflection of truth. That honest relationship can help to break down all the lies we tell ourselves, the social constructs, the programming—the layers that form our identities. For example, a guy might come into our program insisting that everything's fine, but inside he's angry and violent and afraid. The horse senses that and responds accordingly. Then the guy might get angry and blame the horse. But it's not the horse, it's him."

For Micah, this gets at the core of why so many veterans are struggling. "I always tell people, 'You're not the victim of this life. What you're experiencing is your own creation. The horse demonstrates that.' When the individual can stop shifting blame and begin looking at themselves and seeing the direct impact that who they really are is having on the horse, that's when they can begin to fundamentally change. And the lesson becomes all the more powerful because it wasn't spoken with words. So the horses are a tool to help the individual shift from always blaming and looking for answers on the outside to realizing that what they were looking for was already there inside them. When you begin looking inward for answers, instead of relying on the external, you find a true authentic purpose—and this is what allows you to overcome your external circumstances."

The forty-one-day Heroes and Horses program includes intensive skills training, meditation, a whole-foods eating program, a five-hundred-mile wilderness trek, and job placements where participants put what they've learned to use in real-world situations. It's designed to be challenging, raw, and high pressure, because Micah knew that what had helped him the most were the hard days. It was the struggle that had reconnected him with a sense of purpose. He feels that too many programs aimed at veterans are designed to take all the struggle and pain away, or simply to entertain them with vacations and experiences. "The last thing that I needed after a pretty intense special operations career doing the most elite missions possible was to float around in a canoe or go to the Super Bowl," he says. "It's struggle that gives things value."

Since 2013, the program has proven to be so transformative that many graduates come back to volunteer year after year. Applications continue to flood in. The nonprofit recently purchased a 3,500-acre ranch in Montana and is looking to start offering programs year-round, as well as expanding them to include first responders. What drives Micah and his team every day is knowing that, every sixty-two minutes, a veteran takes their own life. And it doesn't have to be that way.

"War is not the problem," Micah says. "Combat does not make you sick or give you a disease. Yes, it's a traumatic experience, and it changes you, like any life experience. But the real problem is the process people encounter when they come home from that experience. They've been programmed in a certain way—how else could a kid who's never even been in a fistfight be turned into a fighter prepared to kill strangers in a country halfway across the world? And then they come home and that programming has no place in our world. They need to be unprogrammed. That's what we're trying to do at Heroes and Horses."

———

The Purpose Is the Journey, Not the Destination

I was honored to be asked to help Micah prepare the mustangs for their five-hundred-mile trek. I believe every horse needs a purpose, and so does every human being. We need a reason to get up in the morning. One of the greatest things we can do for a horse or a human is to help them find their purpose in life, their calling. I saw this project as an opportunity to do just that.

Sometimes it takes us a while to figure out what our purpose is, and sometimes our purpose takes different forms at different stages in life. We may spend years chasing something we think we want, only to discover that it's not satisfying and leaves us disappointed. I used to think my purpose was to be a great polo player. Every day I worked at it, perfecting my timing, my stroke, and my horsemanship skills. I got better and better. Eventually, I found success, winning many prestigious tournaments including the National President's Cup. I loved every minute of that season. But as time passed, I started to realize that playing polo, even becoming a great horseman, wasn't really what I was here to do. The reality is, no matter what you achieve, you can't maintain it forever. There's always a youngster nipping at your heels. And often, when you reach those milestones you imagined would make you happy, they're anticlimactic.

Like Micah, I found my true purpose in serving others. That's where the rewards linger and the sense of satisfaction is truly lasting. I feel that the work I do, using horses to demonstrate this philosophy of life and leadership, is my calling. It's what I was put here on this earth to do. And the horses themselves aren't there to make me look good; it's my job to help them become the best they can be and have a good life. Purpose, as I've come to understand it, isn't a destination out there—a trophy, a number in your bank account, a title. It's a way of living every day.

It's what I see when I look at our border collie, Gracie—she lives to work, and works to live, and she couldn't be happier than when she's doing her job. So many people spend their whole lives chasing some idea of what they want, and in the meantime they're unfulfilled. One of the things I've always admired about cowboys is the way they live a rich life today, enjoying the journey even if all they have is a horse and some cattle.

Micah and the rest of the team had only a few months to prepare their wild mustangs for their epic journey. The first morning, we rose while it was still dark, dressed as warmly as we could, and headed out to the corrals. Micah and I succeeded in separating the big chestnut from the herd, and got him into a round pen with high stock fences. He didn't have a name, so at first we just referred to him by his tag number, 399. Then Micah decided to call him Hambone, in reference to my comment about his big bones. In other parts of the big indoor arena, others were starting to work with their horses, each trainer taking their own approach. I had Micah climb up on top of the fence. The goal was for the horse to bond with him, so I would make myself the source of pressure and see if the horse would choose Micah as his safety.

I've worked with mustangs before, so I knew that the primary issue would be fear. These horses aren't used to being confined or touched in any way, let alone roped and saddled. They've not been raised around people, or seen other horses displaying trust toward humans. In their mind, we're predators, and their experiences during a roundup and at the holding facility probably just confirm this. Their survival instincts are on high alert, and if you corner them, they're liable to try to jump out of the pen, hence the high fences. Horses by nature are claustrophobic and do not like to be trapped in a small area. They have to learn to accept this gradually without force or they tend to become traumatized. I believe freedom is important for all horses, but even more so for the wild ones. You have to give them a lot of space to move their feet, to escape if they need to.

You might have heard of the "fight, flight, or freeze" response. Horses, if given the choice, will choose flight. And it's worked for them—that's how they survived the saber-toothed tiger. We as humans need to allow that flight instinct to play out—something we haven't done well over the centuries in our relationship with the horse. When backed into a corner and offered no way out, horses are given no option but to fight for survival or to freeze up in fear.

I don't want my horses to do either of those things. I don't want them to fight with me, nor do I want them to be paralyzed by fear. It's very important to let the horse know that we are not a predator; we are simply taking on the role of the dominant horse.

You can't force a horse to face his fear. The old cowboys used to try—a process known as "sacking out." They would rope the horse around the neck and use a rope pulley called a "scotch hobble" to lift a hind leg, forcing him to stand on three legs. Then he'd be tied tight to a "snubbing post" in the center of the corral and a tarp or blanket would be thrown repeatedly all over his body and legs. The idea was to make the horse get over his fear of being touched. It didn't hurt him, but it was traumatizing. Being bound up in that way doesn't teach a horse to face or overcome his fear; it just teaches him to freeze up, like a prey animal that goes into a state of shock when it is being devoured by a predator.

A horse that's been trained this way will seem to become accustomed to scary things, but actually the fear has just been driven deep inside. In my experience, that fear will always come back to haunt you at a later date. The horse will never be truly trustworthy. I want the horse to know he can move away freely when he is afraid, and I encourage him to do so—always letting him know he has an escape route. I'd like him to face his fear, but he can choose to do so on his own terms.

Micah had been working with horses for a few years at that point, but he didn't have any experience with wild ones. He'd been taught the old cowboy means of breaking a horse by the tough guys he'd met in the mountains—a process he describes as "quite honestly, a nightmare." I could see he was anxious to learn a new way. Again I was struck by his willingness to humble himself and follow my lead. I take it as a sign of a great leader when they can recognize that someone knows more than they do and not be too proud to learn from them. "If you learn the philosophy of the horse," I advised him, "the rest is just mastering the technique and fitting it to your personality."

I waved my flag and started driving the terrified horse around the pen. When he got close to the big man perched high above him on the fence, he leapt sideways, only to find himself closer to my waving flag. He wheeled around and went the other way. As he got closer to Micah again, I lowered the flag, releasing the pressure. When he spun back toward me, I increased the pressure.

"I want him to realize that being with you is actually the comfortable place, not the pressure place," I explained as the horse slowed down and passed closer to where Micah sat on the fence. "We take the pressure off when he comes up to you, and then increase it when he leaves. Eventually, we want him to feel like the whole world is more pressure than being with you. This is where he'll find his peace." And if Micah's plan worked out, perhaps the horse would find his purpose, too. Out on the trail, crossing mountains and deserts, carrying men and women who were inexperienced and perhaps battling their own inner demons, he'd encounter all kinds of pressure. My job was to teach him to be okay with that, and to find his safety in his relationship with the human in his life.

Some horses are just built for certain kinds of work, mentally and physically. I've had horses I wanted to use for one job that made it quite clear to me they were actually suited for another. Over the years, I like to think I've learned to listen to them better. These mustangs sure seemed suited to the harsh, challenging task of helping veterans find their way back to themselves. I hoped Micah's intuition about this project was right.

The chestnut mustang was full of fear, but he was also brave and smart. I could see him starting to think about the situation he was in, rather than just being reactive. He was figuring out that being with Micah was the better option. He was working on facing his fear. If he could do it, he'd make a good horse for a soldier. The veterans this horse would be helping in his future role would know a lot about fear. They would have been trained to act in the face of sheer terror, to trust their commander and run toward enemy fire even when all their instincts told them to flee. Now those veterans were in a different kind of battle. Their fears were internal, and harder to face. But with the help of horses like this, maybe they could summon up a different kind of bravery out in the wilderness.

The mustang slowed to a walk, and then sidled up right beneath where Micah sat.

"Be very still," I instructed him. "Let the horse come to you." Slowly, Hambone raised his head and tentatively sniffed the man's boot.

"Now lower your hand," I said, "but don't try to touch him. Remember, to him your hand is a claw. It's important to let him touch you first." Gingerly, Micah leaned forward, and the horse nudged his leather-gloved hand.

After some time, when the horse was comfortable standing beside Micah at the fence, I encouraged him to carefully climb down and get in the ring with me. The horse spooked at first when he felt the thud of the man's boots on the ground, and I drove him off, but he quickly came back. I encouraged Micah to get down low. He crouched in the dirt in front of the wild horse, and the horse lowered his head and blew out a big sigh into the man's face.

"It takes a lot to intimidate me," he told me afterward. "That's probably the most vulnerable I've made myself in a long time." At that point, he hadn't been out of the military for very long. He was still, as he puts it, "in a predator mindset," always ready for a fight. The softness required to connect with that horse was something unfamiliar to him—and something he realized was missing in other relationships in his life as well.

When we decided Hambone had done enough for the day,

we went over to see how the others were getting on. One trainer had picked out the best-looking horse in the bunch—a big athletic bay that clearly had better breeding than the rest. He had the horse roped, but it was putting up quite a fight. The other guys gathered around to watch the show.

"You got yourself a tough one," I said. "This one's going to take a lot of time."

"Well, then," one of the guys said, "we should call him Rolex!"

It suited him. Rolex continued to fight at the end of his rope, pinning his ears and digging his heels in, refusing to move. His shaggy coat was dark with sweat and his eyes were glassy with anger. I had my own thoughts about the horse, but didn't want to interfere, so Micah and I went back to our own work. Later, I saw that the guys had given up on Rolex and moved on to an easier prospect. I asked if I could give him another shot. After working with him in the round pen for a while, I was able to get him to relax and stop fighting. Eventually I got him saddled and got on his back. He still needed a lot of time, and I wasn't sure he'd be ready before spring came and it was time to go out on the trail. But if we could put Rolex on a good track, he might just turn out to be as valuable as his name implied.

I headed home, leaving Micah and his team to continue the training. As the weeks passed, Micah progressed to riding Hambone and exposing him to all kinds of pressure—heavy packs, flapping tarps, logs dragged behind him on a rope. He often reminded himself of the three Cs I'd taught him: calm, confident, consistent. The other mustangs, including Rolex, learned similar skills—some training to be riding horses, others to carry packs. By the time I returned, a couple of days before the group's departure, they'd come a long way from the terrified huddle of wild animals I first saw in that pen.

In April 2017, Micah and a handful of other men, including several graduates of the program, set out on their journey with thirteen green-broke mustangs. They'd invited me to go with them, but I couldn't leave Jane to manage the ranch alone for a month while I was in the wilderness. During that month, as spring slowly returned to Wyoming and I went about the business of getting ready for the summer season, I often thought about those men and horses out there on the trail somewhere in New Mexico. Later, I would hear the stories about how they'd crossed the Continental Divide at ten thousand feet in a blizzard, struggled through deserts, gotten lost more than once, and had a collision with a mountain bike that sent a horse and rider headlong into some very spiky cacti. I'd hear the harrowing tale of how Rolex slipped on a steep ascent and went "tumbling ass-over-teakettle down the mountain," in the words of journalist and veteran Elliott Woods, who was one of the party.

"He wound up on his back, his neck pinned under a huge piece of deadfall, his hooves skyward," Woods recalled.* I shuddered to think of that big fighter of a horse in such a precarious position. Amazingly, Rolex had remained calm and trusting

---

* Elliott Woods, "Horse Power: How Wild Mustangs Are Helping Veterans Return to Civilian Life," *Men's Journal,* https://www.mensjournal.com/adven ture/how-horses-helping-veterans-return-civilian-life/.

while the guys rigged a rope around him and hauled and pushed him up, with nothing more than a few scrapes and a swollen eye to show for what could have been a disastrous wreck. Under pressure, that horse really had proven his worth—as had they all. Micah later described that journey, and the months leading up to it, as one of the hardest things he'd ever done—and that's quite a statement from a guy who used to be a Navy SEAL. He also said he learned some of the most valuable lessons of his life, both as a human and as a horseman.

After thirty days, the travelers reached their destination, the once-wild horses now reliable trail partners with five hundred miles behind them. Woods described the arrival at Roosevelt Lake, near Phoenix, Arizona, as being anticlimactic—and that didn't surprise me. After all, the point was never the destination. It's in the journey itself that purpose is found.

CHAPTER TWELVE

Show Your Other Side

Humility is not putting yourself down or denying your strengths; rather, it is being honest about your weaknesses.

—RICK WARREN

D ON'T LET HIM just give you his good side," I told the slender teenage boy standing balanced on the rail of the round pen. The horse in the pen stood close to him, allowing the boy to scratch his neck and around his ear— but only on the left side. "To truly earn his trust means he'll show you both sides—not just the side where he feels confident and secure. He needs to show you the side where he may have been hurt or scared."

The young stallion had already made a huge leap of trust during the hour we'd been working. Never touched by a human hand, he was about a year old. I'd found him in the kill pen at a local auction and decided he deserved another chance. He was a beautiful red roan (a coat color that combines chestnut and white hairs to create a striking pinkish color), so we'd named him Little Red Wrangler. I decided he'd be a good horse to use for a demonstration I was doing that night as part of a birthday celebration for a client. There were about a hundred guests gathered around the pen. I worked with the skittish yearling on some basic boundaries. Then I recruited one of the audience—the teenage boy, whose name was Lucas—to help me teach the horse to trust and be touched.

I used my flag to drive Little Red Wrangler around, but I released the pressure every time he came close to the boy on the fence. *Make the right thing easy and the wrong thing difficult. Honor the slightest try and the smallest change.* Soon, the smart horse had figured out that the boy represented safety and rest and was gravitating toward him, then allowing himself to be touched. But every time I tried to send him in the other direction and get him to allow Lucas to scratch him on the right, the colt spun around. He was only willing to give his left side—his "good side."

Most horses have a "good" side and a "bad" side, a strong side and a weak side. Usually, it means something happened to them on that bad side—something painful or scary that they have a hard time forgetting. When horses cross state lines, they are required to get a blood test, so oftentimes the wild or unbroke ones are driven into a narrow chute and then restrained enough to get a needle into their jugular vein. For a horse like Little Red Wrangler, that might have been his first experience of human contact—the sharp point of a needle entering his neck. He won't forget that. He might get real used to being touched on his left side but still refuse to let you go near the right. The negative experience with the needle was a trigger that makes him more afraid on that side. And that's a problem when you go to get on his back. You always mount a horse from the left, but you've got to swing your leg over to the right side. If it freaks him out when that leg comes into view, you'll end up in the dirt.

It might seem strange that the two sides of a horse could be so different, but it makes sense when you understand how horses see the world. Their eyes are positioned on the sides of their face, not in front, like our eyes. Humans, like cats, dogs, and other predators, have what's known as binocular vision. Our eyes work together to create one three-dimensional image, just like a pair of binoculars focusing. That's great for being able to focus with laser-like precision on what's right in front of you—an important skill if you're hunting for your dinner.

Horses, like cows, deer, and other prey animals, have eyes on the sides of their faces. This gives them a much broader circle of vision—critical for avoiding predators. They can see almost 360 degrees, with the exception of a couple of narrow blind spots. And their eyes work independently, sending separate images to the different sides of the horse's brain (this is known as monocular vision). That's why sometimes a horse can be quite comfortable with you waving a flag on his right side, but then jump out of his skin when you shift it to the other hand and suddenly he sees it in his other eye. It's like a brand-new experience. One side of his brain has already seen it, but the other side has not, and perceives it as a new threat. When working with a horse, it's important to work both sides equally—especially when he's more sensitive about one side, like Little Red Wrangler.

Even though humans are not physically built like horses,

most people I know have a "good" side and a "bad" side, too. There's the side of us that we want to show the world—the side that's confident and has it all figured out. And then there's the side we want to hide—the side where we've been hurt or scared or ashamed or made to feel like a fool. We don't want anyone to see or touch that side. We run around in circles like the colt, making sure our good side is on display and avoiding situations that might expose the stuff we don't want others to see.

I hear from the young people in my life that this is even more true these days with social media. Everyone posts pictures of their best side, with perfect lighting, sharing the highlights of their life. But they don't show the people in their lives their struggles and setbacks. I guess that's natural, and we all do it to some degree. The ranch's Instagram account is all sunset weddings, action shots, and beautiful horses grazing in front of the Tetons. We don't post pictures of the sick cattle we have to doctor, the fences that need fixing, the messes we have to clean up, or the gray and rainy days. I don't imagine anyone wants to see those! But it can be hard work holding up an image and burying other parts of who you are. If you go through life hiding one side of yourself from the world, it can lead to feeling like nobody really knows who you are.

It's also hard work for the people around us. When you have a horse that doesn't want to show you both sides, you end up dancing around him a lot. You know that other side is there, but he's not willing to show it and you're left trying to work around it. I'm sure you know people like that, too. Have you ever been in a situation where everyone was tiptoeing around the leader like they're walking on eggshells, trying to compensate for a weakness or blind spot? Have you ever worked with someone who refused to admit they were wrong, even when it was obvious to everyone else? Have you ever tried to help someone who would only show you their good side, pretending everything is okay even when it's not?

Those relationships are difficult, whether in the workplace, in a family, in a marriage, or in a friendship. We tend to know when someone isn't showing us their whole self, but if they continue to be oblivious, it's hard to trust them. I remember one CEO sent his whole team to the ranch for a day of leadership training, but he didn't come along himself. After the demonstration, more than one person remarked that it was too bad their boss hadn't come—he was the one who needed this message the most.

I'd go so far as to say that if you've only got one side, you don't really have a relationship. And when we hear the stories of leaders who have fallen from grace, so often there seems to be some part of themselves that they were hiding from the public eye until it was dramatically exposed. Of course, I'm not saying we all need to display every aspect of our private lives. But the leaders we trust are those who seem most able to be themselves—to be honest, humble, and transparent—whether in public or in private.

I remember when I first started teaching clinics and doing demonstrations, I felt a tremendous pressure to always appear like I knew what I was doing and to deliver dramatic transformations in the horses. I used to think that I had to get on and ride the horse every time, because that's what people wanted to see. They were paying good money to watch the fearless cowboy. As I got a bit older, however, I found myself hesitating to climb up on some wild young horse I'd just saddled for the first time. After several broken bones, I admit I was more scared of getting bucked off than I used to be. I am older, slower, and more brittle. Plus, I didn't always think the horses were ready. With a few more sessions, they'd have learned to trust more and be more likely to accept a rider calmly. I wasn't a circus act; I was a horse trainer.

"I'm here for the horse first," I told myself.

So one day, I decided to just tell the audience how I felt. I explained to them that I wasn't so keen to get on the horse's back that day. He wasn't ready, I told them, and nor was I. I made a joke about not being as young as I used to be. My wise wife Jane's voice inside my head was telling me, "They don't come with any expectations, so don't take unnecessary risks. You don't have to impress them, they're already impressed." But it was hard for me to get over the idea that I had something to prove.

In fact, I couldn't have been more wrong. People came up to me afterward and told me how much they appreciated my honesty and that they were glad I didn't ride the horse. I'd shown them my other side, and they trusted me all the more for it.

In the summer of 2008, I had a group coming to the ranch that I felt particular pressure to impress. It was a group of leaders from the Federal Reserve—literally some of the most powerful people in the world. This was the highest-profile group I'd worked with up to that time, and I was more nervous than usual. The horse I was planning to use that night had been borrowed from my friend Steven Millward, and I didn't know much about him. But as soon as I got started with the demonstration, I knew it wasn't going to go smoothly. That horse just didn't respond the way most horses do. Perhaps it was some experience in his past. Perhaps he was picking up on my tension. Whatever the reason, he was shut down, hiding his emotions, and unresponsive to my training.

"This isn't working," said the voice in my head as I looked at the faces around the pen. To me, they appeared skeptical, bored, and judgmental, though that may have all been my projection. I was tempted to put more pressure on the horse, to push for a result. But I knew if I got on his back it could all go wrong. And I didn't want to just fake it for the sake of the show.

"Grant," I told myself firmly, "just keep doing the right thing and it will work out. Tell them the truth."

I let the horse be and addressed the audience. "Listen, I'm having trouble getting through to this guy. He's having some issues I don't quite understand, and I think I'm going to need a little more time than normal. Let's take a break, you guys can eat, and then we'll come back to him a little later." All of a sudden, they didn't seem so judgmental after all. I sensed that they appreciated what I'd said.

After they'd had their dinner, they gathered once more around the pen. Within minutes, that horse just melted. He dropped his head, his jaw softened, his eyes started blinking. He went from being hard and angry to being soft and willing. It was just a glimpse of the horse he could be, but it was enough that I did feel ready to get on his back, and he responded with trust.

As I stood beside the horse at the end of the demonstration, I thought about what I'd learned that night. *Do the right thing and it will work out.* I decided to share that message with the Federal Reserve guys. Little did I know what storms were brewing on their horizon that summer. It would be a challenging year, to say the least. They did return to the ranch two other times in the years following the financial crisis, and I was much more relaxed about both of those visits.

Experiences like this have taught me, again and again, the power of simply being authentic. A pedestal is not a safe place to be—when you're balanced up there trying to save face, it's easy to take a tumble. You're much better off with your boots on the solid ground of honesty and transparency. Many of the best and most beloved leaders I've met and worked with over the years demonstrate this truth. They don't hide their own weaknesses, wounds, or fears. They're vulnerable. They share their mistakes and they aren't too proud to admit when they were wrong.

"Humility Comes Before Honor"

One of the most impressive and authentic leaders I've ever had the pleasure of getting to know was a man by the name of Brad Smith. At the time we met, in 2018, he was CEO of the tech company Intuit, who sent a group of their top performers for an award trip in Montana that included my horse-whispering demonstration. Brad and his team were so affected by the experience that I was later invited down to Fort Worth to work with others in the company (including CeCe Morken, whose story I shared in chapter 10).

One of the first things that strikes you on meeting Brad is his broad West Virginia accent—it's not what you'd expect from a Silicon Valley tech leader. But it's a mark of his commitment to authenticity—something he says he learned from his parents.

"Neither my mother nor father had a chance to go to college," he told me. "In fact, my father didn't get to finish high school. But after a lot of trial and error, my father became mayor of our hometown, a little place in West Virginia with a population of three thousand. So I went home one July Fourth holiday and was watching my father give a speech in the town square, with all the red, white, and blue flags flying and people sitting out in their lawn chairs. And in that speech, he used the word *ain't* about twelve times."

Brad recalls that when the speech was over he took his father aside and asked if he was open to a little feedback.

"Of course I am, son," his father replied.

So Brad asked him, "Why would you use the word *ain't* when you won't let my brothers and me do that at the kitchen table?"

His father responded with a question: "Are you trying to help me be better? Or are you embarrassed?" Brad admitted it was a little bit of both.

"Well, son," his father said, "let me help you with something. This is who I am. And if you look around, many of those folks are the same person I am. And maybe if they see me as capable of being the mayor without being perfect, maybe they'll think they could be mayor, too.

"Remember," he added, "people prefer their leaders with flaws. We're our own worst critics, but if we see that someone else who was not perfect can achieve something, then maybe we will believe in ourselves."

Brad credits that example with helping him begin to accept an authentic version of himself. When he began his business career, however, other people weren't always so accepting. One early boss told him his accent made him sound unsophisticated and sent him to a vocal coach. Another supervisor, Brad recalls, "said he was going to coach the folksy out of me." Luckily, it didn't work—and Brad learned that, in the terminology of his industry, "it's not a bug but a feature. It became a distinction, a differentiator, and something that helped me stand out." He's proud of his roots and firm in his belief that one of the most important traits of a leader is authenticity. That means showing all sides of himself—including the "folksy." He's outspoken about his own flaws because he wants them to inspire others.

"I hope people look at me and say, 'Wow. If he can do it and he's that flawed, maybe I can do it, too,'" he says.

Brad showed me the Marshall University class ring he always wears—a Christmas gift from his parents the very day before his father unexpectedly died of a heart attack at the age of just fifty-eight. It reminds him of the commitment and sacrifice his parents made to put their three sons through college, and their pride in that achievement. "My brothers and I wear these rings for two reasons," he says. "Because we had a mommy and a daddy that kept a promise. And because we are proud of where we're from, and it reminds us to pay it forward." One time, he was being photographed for a magazine feature and the photographer asked, "Would you please take the ring off?"

"Why?" Brad asked.

"Because my editor doesn't like bling."

Brad shook his head. "I'm sorry, the ring doesn't come off." It's part of who he is.

Talking to Brad, and seeing him interact with his team, put me in mind of one of my favorite quotes from the Bible: "Humility comes before honor."* He's clearly a leader who people honor and respect, but not because he demands it or puts himself on a pedestal. Quite the opposite. He struck me as a humble and unpretentious man, eager to learn new things. He's also very sensitive to the tone he sets as a leader. When I asked him what lesson had stayed with him from my demonstration, he didn't pick a catchy phrase. He said it was the moment when I got down on my knees in the dirt in front of the horse.

"For me, it really modeled servant leadership," he says, "the idea that the leader's role is to put him- or herself in a vulnerable position and be in service to those that they work with. That changed my entire approach." He also loved the poem "Sermons We See" (shared on pages 10–11), which I recited at the end.

---

* Proverbs 15:33.

"It really struck home for me," he explained, "because one of the things I learned when I first stepped into the role of CEO is all of a sudden, you're six inches taller, your jokes are funnier, you got a little better looking. Everything you do, everything you don't do, even your facial expressions, signal something to the organization, whether you intended them to or not. It's not what you say, it's what you do, where you spend your time, how you react to a crisis, that speaks the loudest to those that you work with. That moment when you recited that poem made me realize that my actions would always speak louder than my words, and I needed to hold myself to that standard."

When Brad decided to retire from his CEO role in 2018, I got the chance to help his team honor their leader. They'd rented the old stockyards in Fort Worth and surprised Brad with a re-enactment of the opening scene from the movie *The Greatest Showman*—with full circus costumes, acrobats, and even a fire-eater. Brad gamely put on the red-and-gold ringmaster's tailcoat and watched the show in amazement, along with several hundred Intuit employees. This was no ordinary retirement party—you could feel the team's genuine love and respect for their leader in the lengths to which they'd gone to honor him. Then they unveiled the next part of the surprise: a horse-whispering demonstration. Looking delighted, Brad came to the side of the round pen we'd set up, still wearing the red-and-gold coat, which made him look kind of like a toy soldier. He warmly shook my hand and Jane's, then took a front-row seat. About six hundred people were sitting up in the stands behind him. I was nervous—this was about as close to a literal circus as I'd ever had to perform in. I knew how much hard work, effort, and expense had gone into this, and I didn't want to blow it.

"Well, here goes," I thought. I took a deep breath, opened my mouth, and started to introduce myself—and quickly realized no one could hear me. Despite all the careful sound checks, my mic was not working. CeCe ran over and gave me her cordless one, and I started over. I worked a two-year-old unbroke filly, giving everyone present the chance to see some of the lessons in action: *Make the right thing easy and the wrong thing difficult. Honor the slightest try and the smallest change. Be slow to take and quick to give. Always quit on a good note.* After the demo, I joined Brad on the stage for a "fireside chat." In our previous meetings, he'd been the one asking me questions; now I was happy that the roles were reversed, and I got the chance to ask him about some of his leadership wisdom. It's a funny thing in my business—people come to me to learn about leadership, but I often find myself learning as much from them, especially the great leaders like Brad. It's not something I expected when I set out on this journey, but something I've come to deeply value.

Don't Mistake Kindness for Weakness

In answer to my opening question, Brad shared his definition of servant leadership: "I've always believed that the definition of leadership is not to put greatness into people, but to recognize that greatness already exists in all of us. Our job is to find a way to let that greatness come out. Servant leadership is putting yourself into service of others to create the environment where they can be natural and be authentic and allow them to discover that beautiful genius that lives inside of them—to instill belief and confidence in the individual that they're the best thing that the world needs, and they just need to be the best version of themselves. And if anything gets in their way, a servant leader's job is to remove those barriers."

"What was the greatest lesson you ever learned about leadership?" I asked Brad. "One that you try to live every day?"

His response was five words: "Don't mistake kindness for weakness." When I asked him to expand on that statement, he came back to the horses. "It's like you said, you can be gentle with the horse but still firm. You don't want to break his spirit. Yes, you need to set boundaries, you need to have respect, but you also need to be kind and let the individual know they're safe around you." It's another lesson he learned from his father.

"One of the things he shared with me is that you can be tough on issues, tough on policy, tough on taxes, whatever, but you always need to be kind to the individual. I never want to think that being a strong leader means being a harsh leader." He also remembered how Intuit's chairman, the legendary coach Bill Campbell, used to say, "Your title makes you a manager, your people will decide if you're a leader." Brad added, "For me, I think the greatest quality that earns leadership is humility."

At the end of our chat, Brad was presented with a beautiful plaque in hand-tooled leather that contained some of his favorite principles from my philosophy. He tells me that to this day, it hangs in his office right alongside the company's values.

I'd be honored to think that I might have influenced a great leader like Brad. But to be honest, I think the reason my philosophy resonated with him so deeply was that it matched up with who he already is. The principles I use to train horses are very similar to the way he led his company, and they were reflected in the culture around him. I might have put them into words in a particular way, and the horses might have helped make those lessons memorable. But in the end, these aren't "my" ideas—they're enduring principles that I've seen in great leaders from all walks of life, as well as great parents, teachers, and coaches. I learn as much from the leaders who come to the ranch as they learn from me—perhaps more.

A Great Leader Knows When to Hand Over the Reins

Brad retired young (though "retirement" is a relative term—he still serves as Intuit's executive chairman). He was just fifty-four when he decided to hand over the reins. "I've always said I knew it would be time to retire when I still had more questions than answers. I never wanted to get to the point where I felt like I had more answers than questions, because no one wants to be around that person and no one can grow around that person, so I want to remain intellectually curious." He also wanted to pursue other ways in which he felt called to serve, including the founding of a nonprofit, the Wing 2 Wing Foundation, to promote entrepreneurship and equal opportunity in his home region of Appalachia.

Being a part of Brad's retirement put me in mind of another of the best leaders I know, who is also nearing retirement: Freckles. My faithful companion is now twenty-six years old, and he has been leading his herd and partnering with me in demonstrations for longer than Brad led Intuit. These days, his coat is almost pure white and his back is beginning to sag a little. When I first met Freckles, he was three years old and his coat was a dark iron gray. People who meet him now don't believe this, until I show them a picture that's hanging in the barn.

I often ask myself when the time will come for Freckles to retire. I hope he'll tell me when he's ready, or I hope I'll be wise enough to know. Freckles loves his job and is so good at it that I don't know how I'll ever replace him. He doesn't just help with the corporate demonstrations; he loves weddings as well. He's famous for sticking his head into the photos and trying to steal the limelight from the groom. Photographers swear he understands their instructions and poses.

He's also a great leader for the other horses. He knows that kindness is not a sign of weakness, and he's gentle but firm with the youngsters. The herd will follow him just about anywhere, but they have to stay behind him, so they all go pretty slow these days. People ask me, "What are you going to do when Freckles retires?" I reply, "I'm going to retire, too!" A truly great, authentic servant leader like Freckles is hard to find, and even harder to replace.

But like Brad, I'm not really done yet. I, too, still feel called to serve. And I look forward to the day when I can pass the torch to the next generation—when the ceiling of my life becomes a platform on which my and Jane's children and grandchildren can stand. The timeless beauty of the land on which we live has nurtured generation after generation, and I believe that the principles we teach here and the impact they have on people's lives will also outlast us. Like the majestic Tetons, I hope they will go on to inspire and uplift, long after I've hung up my spurs.

ACKNOWLEDGMENTS

I will always be indebted to the great horsemen from whom I learned the philosophy and many of the practices that I share in this book: Ray Hunt, for showing me a better way; Tom Dorrance, for his humble wisdom; Tink Elordi, for his patience in working with me; David Gonzales, for his mentorship; and William Devane, for introducing me to Ray Hunt.

I am grateful to have found a writing partner, Ellen Daly, who was a joy to work with, while also guiding the project with great professionalism and expertise. She had a knack for capturing my voice and bringing out the essence of each story. I am also thankful to Jaime Feary, who helped me with my first book and whose storytelling skill is also reflected in these pages.

This book would not have come into being without my stepson Luke Long, who has been a champion of the idea from day one and was a driving force behind making it a reality. Our good friend Cody H. Carolin has been equally instrumental, and I'm grateful for her support and insight.

Acknowledgments

On the publishing front, I've been blessed with a wonderful team. My agent, Jim Levine, saw the potential in this project early on, and guided it with a steady hand to a horse-loving editor at Putnam, Michelle Howry, who has been sensitive and wise in her editorial suggestions. I've also appreciated the care and expertise of Courtney Paganelli, Ashley Di Dio, and the teams at Levine Greenberg Rostan and Penguin Random House.

The beauty of the ranch has always attracted talented photographers, many of whom have become friends. Chris Douglas came into our life as we were just getting started with the work we do and has been part of our life on and off ever since. We are grateful for his contribution to this book. A picture speaks a thousand words, and we couldn't have asked for a better cover image than Andy Bardon's striking photograph. Carly Butler, John Balsom, and Hector Perez have also captured the spirit of my work through their lenses.

Above all, I am thankful for my family. My children—Tara, Luke, and Peter—who have taught me so much about how the lessons I've learned from the horses can apply to parenting as well. My daughters-in-law, Lauren and Kirby, and my grandchildren, Atlas and Walter, who give me hope and inspiration for the future. And my wife, Jane, whose consistence, insistence, and persistence has made this book possible.

Lastly, my deepest gratitude to all whose stories are shared in these pages, both horses and humans. It's the transformations I witness every day that inspire me to keep doing what I do. You made this book worth writing—and, I hope, worth reading.

PHOTO CREDITS

Photos on pages iv, 34, 52, 172, and 188 courtesy of Chris Douglas.

Photos on pages 14, 136, and 154 courtesy of Andrew J. Bardon.

Photo on page 70 courtesy of John Balsom.

Photos on pages 96 and 232 courtesy of Carly Butler Photography.

Photo on page 112 courtesy of Hector Perez.

Photos on pages xii and 210 courtesy of author.

INDEX

abused horses, 56, 131
alertness of horses, 20, 43
allegorical aspects of horse training, 8
anger/rage of horses, 116–17, 162–63, 168
attitude
   and bucking of horses, 162–63,
     167–71
   dealing with an attitude, 160–64,
     165–66
   infectious quality of, 165
   and laying horses down, 169–70
auctions, "kill pens" at, 175–76, 182, 235
authenticity
   inspiring, in others, 32
   power of, 239–42
   and servant leadership, 248
   Smith's commitment to, 242–45
   trust inspired by, 239

Balsom, John, 45–49
Balzhiser, Dave, 40–41
battles of will, 105–7
body language
   behaviors telegraphed by, 161, 169
   beliefs translated into, 58
   distinguishing anger and fear in, 162
   establishing respect, 170

and "having feel" for horses, 39
and saddle training horses, 46–47
sensitivity to, 42–45
and social order among horses, 76
border collies, 85
boundaries, 71–95
   applied softly and firmly, 84–85, 86,
     93–94
   consequences of poor, 84
   failure to establish, 78–82
   and freedom to choose, 89, 90–93,
     95, 103
   between horses and humans, 6, 83–84
   horses' responsiveness to, 20
   impact of pandemic on, 79
   importance of clear, 85–86, 90
   of parents with children, 79, 80–82,
     91–92, 93–94
   power to unite, 94–95
   respect as related to, 79, 80, 86–90
   sense of safety fostered by, 32, 79, 95
   and social order in herds of horses,
     74–78, 79, 95
   testing of, 94
   trust's relationship to, 79, 86–87, 94
Braveheart, 55–58, 62–69
Buchanan, Mike, 20–21

Index

bucking of horses
  addressing, 106, 117, 167–71
  and fear of riders, 121
  of first-time colts, 167
  and horses bred for sport, 140
  and laying horses down, 169–70
  and tantrums of horses, 116–17,
    162–63, 168–69
  telegraphed by horses, 44, 120
  triggered by riders' restraint, 101
  and trust between horse and rider, 121
bullies, 83

Campbell, Bill, 248
children/youth
  bad attitudes imitated by, 165
  expressions of fear in, 162
  importance of boundaries for, 79,
    80–82, 91–92, 93–94
  importance of discipline for, 159
  lacking a solid foundation, 153
  power of language/labels with, 58–62
  rewarding wrong choices of, 106
choices, freedom in making, 24–25, 26,
  89, 90–93, 108–9
comfort zone, lack of growth in, 204–6
compassion, 32
Concho's lessons in respect, 76–78
confidence
  building, 24, 39, 152, 171
  and freedom to move, 101
  and good/bad sides of horses, 235, 238
  importance of boundaries for, 77,
    79, 91
  and servant leadership, 248
  undermining, 118
Conroy, Jim, 200
consequences, applying, 90–93
convicts' work at Honor Farm, 20–21
COVID-19 pandemic, 79, 206–7
cowboy poetry, 10–11, 142–43, 143n
cowboys' sense of fulfillment, 223

danger, horses' instincts for, 20–21
discipline, importance of, 158, 159–60
Dorrance, Tom, 7, 39, 44, 86, 87, 171

Elordi, Tink
  on Braveheart's progress, 64
  on building on the good, 171
  on "feel," 37–38, 39, 40
  "hang in there" advice of, 106–7
  influence on author, 7, 44
  on prioritizing the horse, 142
  emotional intelligence, 40. *See also* feel
expectations, 58–62
eyes and vision of horses, 237

failure
  fear of, 194–98, 200
  freedom to experience, 199–200
  learning from, 191–94, 195–98,
    200–201, 204
  role of, in progress, 197–98
  willingness to risk, 204–6
fairness, 6
faults, facing, 22, 42
fears
  Braveheart's overcoming of, 55–58,
    62–69
  and bucking of horses, 162
  and conventional horse training,
    224–25
  countering, with freedom to choose,
    24–25
  as expressed by young people, 162
  of failing, 194–98, 200
  and fight, flight, or freeze response,
    224
  and flight tendencies of horses, 24,
    224
  and good/bad sides of horses, 235–37
  as habit, 206
  overshadowing strengths, 24
  and process of building trust, 130
  responding to mistakes born of,
    194–95
  turning to face, 24–25, 195, 226–27
  of wild mustangs, 223–24
Federal Reserve, U.S., 240–42
feel, 35–50
  about, 39–40
  continually trying to, 50

256

development of, 39, 40–42
reading body language, 42–45
fight, flight, or freeze response, 224
Fink, Micah, 213–21
and Heroes and Horses, 213–15,
219–21, 222–30
on horses' role in reflecting truth,
219–20
military training/service of, 217
sense of purpose, 220
on struggles of veterans, 218, 219–20,
221
and terrorist attacks of September 11,
2001, 216–17
firmness in approach, 84–85, 86,
93–94, 160
flight tendencies of horses, 24, 224
force, training/relationships based on,
38, 44, 108–11
forgiveness, 48–49, 67–69
foundation, building/rebuilding a strong,
100–101, 140–44, 150, 151–53
Freckles, 77–78, 81, 84, 100–101, 111,
250–51
freedom to choose
as applied by leaders, 102–3, 108–9
countering fears with, 24–25
fostering trust with, 24–25, 26
and respecting boundaries, 89,
90–93, 95, 103
restraint-free approach of author,
101–2
and rider–horse relationship, 100–102
and wild horses, 224, 225

good/bad sides
of horses, 236–37
of humans, 237–39
Gupta, Rajneesh, 203
"The Guy in the Glass" (Wimbrow), 21

harm, avoiding doing, 122, 160
Headspace Inc., 206–8
Helms, James, 201, 202
herds of horses, social order in, 74–78,
79, 95

Heroes and Horses, 213–15, 219–21,
222–30
Honor Farm, 20–21
horse whispering, 6
humbling horses, 169–70
humility
and creating safe environments, 32
as leadership quality, 248
and leadership training, 201, 203
and leading with feel, 50
in response to respect, 18
and willingness to learn, 225
Hunt, Ray, 6, 7, 38–39, 44, 99,
103, 197

intentions, horses' ability to sense,
20–21
Intuit, 191–93, 198–99, 200–203,
243–50
intuition, trusting, 49

James Dean (JD), 157–64
Jubal, 145–48, 150, 151–52, 153
judging others, 31–32

Keith (ranch hand), 199–200
"kill pens" at horse auctions, 175–76,
182, 235
kindness, 4, 248
Knox, Jack, 85

language/labels, power of, 57–62
laying horses down, 169–70
leaders
authenticity in, 239
and boundaries, 76
and earning trust, 125
exercising vulnerability, 245
and freedom to choose, 102–3,
108–9
and humility, 225, 248
and picking one's battles, 107–8
servant leadership, 125, 208, 245,
247–48
takeaways from demonstrations,
122–23

learning
 failure/mistakes as a means to,
  191–94, 195–98, 200–201, 204
 and leading with feel, 50
 uncomfortable process of, 41–42
 willingness to engage in, 50, 225
Legs, 168–71
Little Red Wrangler, 235–36, 237
living what one has learned, 22–24, 30,
  31, 32
long-term outlook, 24, 32, 141,
  150, 153
loyalty, 108, 109, 111

Makowicz, Dave, 115–16, 123
Milagro, 175–80, 181, 182
Millward, Steven, 183–87, 241
mirrors, horses' ability to act as, 20–22,
  219–20
mistakes, willingness to make, 191–94,
  195–98, 204–6
monocular vision of horses, 237
Morken, CeCe, 191–93, 198–99,
  200–203, 206–8
Morris, Jeremy
 employment at ranch, 18–19
 leadership of, 30
 on recovery from failure, 198
 self-destructive behaviors of, 19,
  26–28, 29–30
 sobriety of, 30
 wounds carried by, 18, 25, 26, 28–29,
  30–31
mules, training, 3–4
mustangs, wild
 fearfulness of, 223–24
 and Heroes and Horses program,
  213–15, 221, 223, 225–30
 and Honor Farm program, 21
 training, 225–28
 Wildfire's training, 17–18, 22–23, 25

names, power/importance of, 57–58
natural horsemanship, 6
Neal (ranch hand), 125–29

observation, importance of, 161
ownership, personal, 218

parents
 boundary setting of, 79, 80–82,
  91–92, 93–94
 and disciplining children, 159
 and power of language/labels, 58–62
partnership, relationships based on force
  vs., 108–11
patience, 4, 32
picking one's battles, 107–8
poetry, cowboy, 10–11, 142–43, 143*n*
pressure and release, application of
 and attitude in colts, 167, 169
 in bonding exercises, 223, 225–26, 236
 effectiveness of, 7
 in establishing boundaries, 93
 and honoring small tries/changes,
  121–22, 199
 incremental increases in, 85, 92, 171
 in making right choices, 18, 85, 101,
  107, 195
 triggers that create pressure, 181
 using a flag in, 117, 195, 225, 236
 using noise in, 89, 91
 with verbal communication, 85
prey animals, horses as
 and alertness of horses, 20, 43
 and monocular vision of horses, 237
 and sensitivity of horses, 20
pride, 196
principles/philosophy of author's
  approach
 about, 10, 19
 and author's mentors, 44
 *being as soft as you can, but as firm as
  necessary,* 84–85, 86, 93–94, 160
 don't be afraid to move your feet, 204, 207
 *honoring the slightest try and smallest
  change,* 118, 119–24, 130, 148, 150,
  199, 236
 *if you deal with an attitude, you don't
  have to deal with an action,* 160–64,
  165–66

it's not about today; it's about the rest of their lives, 24, 32, 141, 150, 153
making the right thing easy and the wrong thing difficult, 17–18, 89, 103–5, 106, 109, 148, 195, 236
quitting on a good note, 47, 64, 122, 143
respect before friendship, 80, 88, 89, 148
slow to take and quick to give, 118, 119, 122, 127, 148, 153
progress
  acknowledgement of, 118
  role of failure/mistakes in, 197–98
  trusting in, 62–67
punishment, 117, 194–95
purpose
  about, 222–23
  found on the journey of daily life, 222, 230
  and Heroes and Horses program, 214, 219–20
  horses' need for, 214, 221, 226
  searching for a sense of, 221–22
  in serving others, 222
  veterans' search for, 214, 219

reflecting/revealing truth, horses' instincts for, 20–22, 219–20
resentment, 67, 102, 108, 109, 122, 165
resistance, 130
respect
  and basic principles of author, 4
  and body language, 170
  before friendship, 80, 88, 89, 148
  horses with lack of, 158–59
  humility in response to, 18
  mutual, 6
  role of boundaries in, 79, 80, 86–90
responsibility, personal, 218
restraint-free approach of author, 101–2
rewards
  for making a right choice, 116–18, 119–24
  releasing pressure, 85, 93, 117, 199
  for risk taking, 192

for small signs of progress, 8, 47, 118, 130
for wrong behavior, 107
risks, willingness to take, 191–94, 204–6
Rooster, 99–101, 102, 103, 104–5
running of horses, 24–25

"sacking out" process, 224–25
safety, sense of
  and acknowledgement of change, 118
  environments that foster, 25–26, 31–32
  importance of transparency to, 42
  prioritized over risk of failure, 196, 204–5
  role of boundaries in, 32, 79, 95
  in round pen, 24
  and social order among horses, 74
selling horses, 38
sensitivity of horses
  and approaches that protect trust, 119
  to attitudes/intentions of riders, 58, 219
  and disciplining horses, 84
  as prey animals, 20, 43
September 11, 2001, terrorist attacks, 216–17
"Sermons We See" (Guest), 10–11, 245
shortcomings, acknowledgement of, 21–22, 42
Smith, Brad, 242–50
  commitment to authenticity, 242–45
  on flaws, 244
  on lessons in leadership, 248
  retirement of, 246–47, 249–50
  on servant leadership, 245, 247–48
social justice, 207
social media, 238
social order in herds of horses, 74–78, 79, 95
softness in approach, 39, 84–85, 86, 93–94, 160
spoiled horses, 78, 87–89, 116
Story, Steve, 140, 144–50, 151
submitting to leadership, 130–31

tantrums of horses, 116–17, 162–63, 168–69
terrorist attacks of September 11, 2001, 216–17
tragedies, good outcomes from, 183–87
training mules/horses
  and bucking of horses, 106
  and fear of breaking horses' spirit, 170
  and good/bad sides of horses, 236–37
  horse-led approach to, 6
  and mounting a horse for the first time, 46–47
  old methods of, 3–4, 6, 46, 106, 225
  and rewarding good choices, 116–18, 119–24
  role of trust in, 46–47, 120–21
  transparency in demonstrations of, 240–42
  wild mustangs, 225–28
transparency, 32, 42, 239–42
trauma, 20, 131–34
triggers, 23, 31
trust
  and acknowledgement of progress, 117–18
  approaches that protect and build, 119
  and authenticity in leaders, 239
  and basic principles of author, 4
  in training horses, 46–47, 120–21
  earning, 125–29
  expressed by horses, 25
  failures of, 65–67
  fostering an environment of, 25–26
  foundational importance of, 26, 124
  and freedom to choose, 24–25, 26
  and "having feel" for horses, 39
  and leadership training, 201
  mutual, 6, 120–21
  and overcoming trauma, 131–34

process of building (acronym), 130–31
real-world implications of, 142
role of boundaries in, 79, 86–87, 94
truth, horses' ability to reflect/reveal, 20–22, 219–20

understanding, 130
U.S. Federal Reserve, 240–42

Velvet's lesson in boundaries, 87–89
veterans
  building trust following trauma, 131–34
  and Heroes and Horses program, 213–15, 219–21, 222–30
  regaining a sense of purpose, 214, 219
  struggles of, 131, 217, 218, 219–20, 221, 226–27

weaknesses
  facing, 22
  mistaking kindness for, 248
wild horses
  alertness of, 43
  allowing a sense of freedom to, 224, 225
  fearfulness of, 87
  See also mustangs, wild
Woods, Elliott, 229
work ethic, establishing, 163–64
wounds
  carried by Jeremy, 18, 25, 26, 28–29, 30–31
  carried by John, 45–49
  compassion for invisible, 32
  dangers of not facing, 31
  unconscious cues of, 45–49

youth. *See* children/youth
youth of author, 3–4, 118